THE GREAT GATSBY

Craig's Notes
Classroom Guide

Candace R. Craig

Copyright 2014 by Candace R. Craig©. All rights reserved. No part of this publication may be reproduced, stored in a retrieval system, or transmitted in any way or by any means (electronic, mechanical, photocopying, recording, or otherwise) without prior written permission from Candace R. Craig, with the following exceptions: CreateSpace, an Amazon Company and Amazon Kindle Direct Publishing for publication and distribution, photocoping of student worksheets by a teacher who purchased this publication for his/her own class is permissible. Reproduction of any part of this publication for an entire school or for a school system or for commercial sale is strictly prohibited. Copyright infringement is a violation of federal law.

THE GREAT GATSBY

Table of Contents

A Letter to the Teacher 4
Pre-Reading Activities 5
The Socio-Historical and Political Context Quest 6
About the Author Quest 9

Chapter One
- Pre-Reading Prompts and Vocabulary 12
- Post-Reading, Pre-Discussion Quiz 14
- Pre-Discussion Critical Summary for the Teacher 16
- Class Reading Activity: At the "Tom Buchanans" 17
- Characterization Activity 22
- Post-Discussion Quest 23

Chapter Two
- Pre-Reading Prompts and Vocabulary 25
- Post-Reading, Pre-Discussion Quiz 26
- Pre-Discussion Critical Summary for the Teacher 27
- Imagery: A Drawing Activity 29
- Post-Discussion Quest 30

Chapter Three
- Pre-Reading Prompts and Vocabulary 31
- Post-Reading, Pre-Discussion Quiz 33
- Pre-Discussion Critical Summary for the Teacher 35
- Reading Images as Text Activity 37
- Post-Discussion Quest 39

Chapter Four
- Pre-Reading Prompts and Vocabulary 42
- Post-Reading, Pre-Discussion Quiz 44
- Pre-Discussion Critical Summary for the Teacher 46
- Setting: Map Activity 49
- Post-Discussion Quest 51

Chapter Five
- Pre-Reading Prompts and Vocabulary 53
- Post-Reading, Pre-Discussion Quiz 54
- Pre-Discussion Critical Summary for the Teacher 55
- Symbol Activity 57
- Post-Discussion Quest 58

THE GREAT GATSBY

Chapter Six
- Pre-Reading Prompts and Vocabulary 60
- Post-Reading, Pre-Discussion Quiz 61
- Pre-Discussion Critical Summary for the Teacher 62
- Recurring Motif Activity 64
- Post-Discussion Quest 65

Chapter Seven
- Pre-Reading Prompts and Vocabulary 67
- Post-Reading, Pre-Discussion Quiz 69
- Pre-Discussion Critical Summary for the Teacher 70
- Situational Irony Activity 73
- Post-Discussion Quest 74

Chapter Eight
- Pre-Reading Prompts and Vocabulary 75
- Post-Reading, Pre-Discussion Quiz 77
- Pre-Discussion Critical Summary for the Teacher 78
- Character Foil Activity 83
- Class Reading Activity: George Wilson 85
- Post-Discussion Quest 88

Chapter Nine
- Pre-Reading Prompts and Vocabulary 90
- Post-Reading, Pre-Discussion Quiz 92
- Pre-Discussion Critical Summary for the Teacher 94
- Allusion Activity 98
- The Effect of a Comparison Activity 99
- Post-Discussion Quest 100

Culminating Discussion Questions 103

Five Elements of Plot Construction 104

Essay Topics 105

Twenty Post-Reading Creative Project Ideas 106

Answer Keys for Quizzes & Quests 116

THE GREAT GATSBY

Classroom Guide

Dear Fellow Teacher,

Whether you are new to teaching in the literature classroom or a veteran, I write this guide for you. I have been teaching literature and humanities, particularly American Literature, since 2000. While I believe the deepest and most enduring classroom experiences are rooted in the teacher's own intimacy with and passion for the texts at the center of each study unit, I know something else: teachers spend many hours reading and rereading, analyzing texts for literary terms and discussion material, creating quizzes and tests, and embarking upon all-consuming searches for the best, most age-appropriate and differentiated activities amenable to all the learning modalities. If you are a new teacher, either to the general literature classroom or to something more accelerated, like Advanced Placement English Language or Literature, the task is even more daunting, however rewarding.

This teacher's guide is a collection of tested ideas, activities, and more, from my multiple years of teaching *The Great Gatsby* in both the AP and the non-AP classrooms. It is not meant to replace you and your own ideas, but to help you maximize your experience teaching the novel. Take what you need and save the rest for another time. To prepare the guide, I have revisited my own original tests, quizzes, ideas, etc., and edited out those activities and questions that seemed a little like red herrings for the highly capable student and revised others for better clarity. I reread my old, well-annotated copy of the novel and wrote critical summaries for all chapters, drawing upon my repeated engagements with the novel throughout the years. The commentary in these summaries is directly related to the class discussion questions and material covered on the quizzes and quests. Page numbers in all citations are from my old Scribner's 2004 copy of the novel. However, the pagination was up to date at the time of this publication.

Included in these critical summaries is advice for the teacher concerning what barriers my students often faced in trying to grasp the more abstract suggestions. I have also added links to reputable websites with superb ideas for teaching important concepts and literary devices. So, I have done much of the tedious legwork for you. Check out my contents page to get a sense of the range of teacher materials I've created specifically for Fitzgerald's most famous novel. Moreover, use this guide to launch one of the best experiences you will ever have as a teacher of literature: leading students through their first encounter with *The Great Gatsby*!

"And so we beat on . . . ."

Candace

THE GREAT GATSBY

Pre-Reading Activities

I have used some great videos to review key events of the Roaring Twenties. One is from *History.com*. It is called *America, The Story of Us: "Boom"*. It is from the History Channel at http://www.history.com/shows/america-the-story-of-us/videos and it is from a series of videos chronicling major events in America's history, from the Revolution to the modern day. Like the rest of the videos in the series, *Boom* is about 45 minutes in length. You can also find it on YouTube for free. If you go the YouTube route, you can easily use it as a flipped classroom homework assignment.

As I am a big fan of Ken Burns, I should mention a couple of wonderful related documentaries. One is *Prohibition*. You'll need to select out episodes you think work best as an introduction to the political policies that provide the backdrop for the novel. I should also mention his documentary, *Jazz*. Episodes 2 and 3 are concerned with the 1920s, but, again, you'll want to pick and choose the segments carefully, as even the segments within the episodes, themselves, may not work for you. Here is the link to the PBS *Jazz* episode guide:
http://www.pbs.org/jazz/about/about_behind_the_scenes4.htm.

As always, check out PBS.org and enter your search term. These videos ought to be available for streaming through your respective personal and school accounts (i.e., *Netflix*, *Amazon*, etc.).

Pre-Reading Journal Writing

Write a journal entry on one of the following topics:

1. Some people believe that you cannot truly have a good life without a good deal of money. Do you agree? What are the advantages and possible disadvantages of having great wealth?

2. Have you ever dreamed of doing something great, but that other people thought was silly or a pipedream? Explain. What was your reaction to them? Do you agree with them now? Why or why not?

3. Discuss the notion of "The American Dream." Traditionally, what were the goals of our forefathers, and how were they to be achieved? Although everyone has a right to live the American dream, are all people equal in their ability to turn this right into a reality? Explain.

THE GREAT GATSBY

The Socio-Historical and Political Context   Name_____

Directions: Do some online research to answer the following questions about the context of *The Great Gatsby*. Be sure to keep track of the sources that provide you with your answers (Look at the final page to see why.). Try to stick with sites that end in *.org*, *.gov* or *.edu*:

_____1. The phrase, "Coolidge Prosperity" refers to
   A. The Prosperity of Calvin Coolidge himself.
   B. The seven years of prosperity in American from 1923-1929, during which time Calvin Coolidge was president.
   C. To anyone who seems to be lucky in business, we say, "You are filled with Coolidge Prosperity."
   D. The title of Calvin Coolidge's autobiography

_____2. What 1920's figure tended to set the standard of ethics and behavior during this time?
   A. The priest
   B. The philosopher
   C. The businessman
   D. The statesman

_____3. What new model of car was introduced in December of 1927 and caused a great buzz in major cities all across America?
   A. Harry Carey's personal custom-built phaeton.
   B. Henry Ford's Model T
   C. Robin's-egg-blue Chevrolets
   D. Henry Ford's Model A

_____4. Many middle-class Americans in the 1920s owned all of the following, **EXCEPT**
   A. A Refrigerator
   B. A Car
   C. A Television
   D. A Radio
   E. Indoor plumbing

_____5. What made the United States so prosperous during this time?
   A. It had developed mass production and managerial efficiency.
   B. World War 1 did not impoverish American like it did other places, such as Europe.
   C. America had enormous resources in materials and human energy.
   D. All of the above made the United States prosperous.

THE GREAT GATSBY

_____6. "The Consumer" became another major figure during this time. All of the following were put into practice in order to get people to exercise their purchasing power, **EXCEPT**
   A. Advertising and competition
   B. Psychology
   C. Low-pressure sales strategies
   D. The encouragement of stock market speculation
   E. Opportunities to purchase items on credit.

_____7. Which of the following was becoming less of a popular amusement during the Coolidge years?
   A. The Motion Picture
   B. Activities found at municipal parks and recreation centers
   C. The phonograph
   D. Railroad excursions with family
   E. A romantic weekend car ride with your date

_____8. Which is NOT true about the flourishing of jazz?
   A. It was spread into wider public consumption through the radio and the phonograph.
   B. It originated in its most incipient[1] form in New Orleans and then expanded North and East.
   C. F. Scott Fitzgerald wrote the new jazz music for his famous musical called, _The Jazz Age_.
   D. Duke Ellington and Mamie Smith were two of its major figures.

_____9. All of the following are characteristics common to "the flapper" girl, **EXCEPT**
   A. Confident, independent, and sometimes a bit vulgar
   B. Wears heavy make-up and is not afraid to apply lipstick in public
   C. Scantily dressed, compared to her mother; can light up a cigarette with abandon and ease.
   D. Decisive and focused about everything.

_____10. The bootlegger is
   A. A man who makes boots that will fit the length of a man's leg so that he may transport liquor.
   B. One who makes, smuggles, and sells liquor illegally.
   C. A man who hides his liquor in the leg of his boot in order to transport it.
   D. An authority figure that empties beer barrels of their contents onto the street.
   E. Both A and B
   F. Both B and C

---
[1] Infantile, budding, early.

THE GREAT GATSBY

_____11. Who was George Remus?
- A. A famous bootlegger
- B. The son of German immigrants and an example of the new breed of American during the 1920s.
- C. A man of many professions
- D. None of the Above
- E. All of the Above

DIRECTIONS: Do the following on a separate sheet of paper:

12. What was the 19th Amendment, and when was it passed? What effect did the passing of this law have upon Americans or America? List three answers:

13. What was the 18th Amendment, and when was it passed? What effect did the passing of this law have upon Americans or America? List three answers

Write down the sources you used to get ALL of the above information. For each source, include (A) the name of the author by last name first (if there is one), (B) the title of the individual section you read, and (C) the title of the website, itself. Number each source.

THE GREAT GATSBY

About the Author   Name_____

Directions: Do online research to answer the following questions on the life of F. Scott Fitzgerald. Be sure to keep track of the sources that gave you your answers (see the final page). Try to stick with sources that end in *.org*, *.edu* or *.gov*:

_____1. F. Scott Fitzgerald was born in
  A. Montgomery, Alabama
  B. St. Louis, Missouri
  C. St. Paul, Minnesota
  D. Chicago, Illinois
  E. None of the Above

_____2. As a boy, Fitzgerald was
  A. Extremely poor
  B. Very popular
  C. Class conscious
  D. Extremely rich
  E. None of the Above

_____3. Fitzgerald's earliest creative writings were published in
  A. School Magazines
  B. Scribner's
  C. *The Tiger*
  D. *Nassau Library*
  E. None of the Above

_____4. Fitzgerald attended
  A. Yale
  B. Harvard
  C. Princeton
  D. Columbia
  E. None of the Above

_____5. Which of the following women was NOT a romantic interest for Fitzgerald?
  A. Jordan Baker
  B. Ginerva King
  C. Zelda Sayre
  D. Sheilah Graham

_____6. Which one of the following sentences did Fitzgerald use to describe his wife?
  A. Her voice was full of money.

THE GREAT GATSBY

   B. I was in love with a whirlwind, and I must spin a net big enough to catch it out of my head.
   C. Her face was sad and lovely with bright things in it, bright eyes and a bright passionate mouth.
   D. None of the Above

_____7. Fitzgerald wrote all of the following, **EXCEPT**
   A. *This Side of Paradise*
   B. *The Beautiful and Damned*
   C. *The Sun Also Rises*
   D. *Tender is the Night*

_____8. All is true of the Fitzgeralds, **EXCEPT**
   A. They embodied the spirit of the Jazz Age.
   B. They dived into the fountain at the Plaza Hotel.
   C. They hit a woman accidentally when the woman suddenly ran out into the road.
   D. They rode on the hoods of taxi cabs down Fifth Avenue in NYC.
   E. All of the above are true.

_____9. The courtship between Daisy and Gatsby in *The Great Gatsby* is based most strikingly upon
   A. Fitzgerald's relationship to Zelda
   B. Fitzgerald's relationship to Ginerva
   C. Fitzgerald's relationship to Sheilah
   D. Both A and B
   E. Both A and C

_____10. The Fitzgeralds lived for a while as expatriates in what European country?
   A. England
   B. France
   C. Germany
   D. Spain
   E. None of the Above

_____11. Later in life, Zelda was diagnosed with
   A. Cancer
   B. Polio
   C. Schizophrenia
   D. None of the Above

_____12. Throughout his adult life, Fitzgerald was addicted to
   A. Opium
   B. Alcohol
   C. Amphetamines (Uppers)

THE GREAT GATSBY

    D. Pain killers
    E. None of the Above

_____13. Fitzgerald died at the age of 44 of
    A. A drug overdose
    B. A heart attack
    C. Lung cancer
    D. Liver failure

_____14. Fitzgerald's wife died from
    A. Suicide
    B. A car accident in which she drove over a cliff
    C. A terrible fire
    D. A drug overdose
    E. None of the Above

_____15. Fitzgerald was working on which one of the following novels when he died?
    A. *The Crack Up*
    B. *Tender is the Night*
    C. *The Last Tycoon*
    D. *Winter Dreams*
    E. He wasn't working on anything when he died.

DIRECTIONS: Use a separate sheet of paper to do the following:

Write down the sources you used to get the above information. For each source, include (A) the name of the author by last name first (if there is one), (B) the title of the individual section you read, and (C) the title of the website, itself. Number each source. You may get extra points for using sites that end with *.edu* or *.org*. Your teacher will decide the specifics.

THE GREAT GATSBY

Chapter One

Pre-Reading Journal Questions:

1. If you could move anywhere in the world for just one year, where would you go? Why?
2. What sorts of qualities make for a good friend? Give reasons.

Vocabulary Review: In chapter one, you will encounter the following words. For each word, find its definition and write a sentence using the word correctly. Be sure there is enough information in your sentence so your teacher can tell that you understand *how* the word is used. **Do not simply repeat the word's definition in your sentence.** Identify its part of speech as written below (i.e., adjective, noun, verb, adverb):

- Supercilious
- Fractiousness
- Contemptuously
- Bantering
- Extemporizing
- Characterization (literary term)

Preview of Class Discussion:

1. **Clarify** what you learned from chapter one about each of the following characters: Nick, Tom, Jordan, and Daisy.

2. How does Nick's role differ from that of the other characters? How will this affect how you get to know the other characters from here on out? Do you think Nick will be a reliable narrator? If yes or no, then what words from chapter one drive your assumptions?

3. What **assumptions** can you make about each one of these characters based upon what you learned about them in chapter one? Provide a quote or passage of **evidence** that supports your assumptions.

4. How might each of the characters' **viewpoints** of themselves differ from your own viewpoint of them? Why might they differ?

5. Based upon what you know about these characters so far, how do you think the situation brewing between all of them will progress further into the novel? Do you have any predictions for one or more of these characters? What **reasons** do you have for these predictions? Refer to words, phrases, descriptions, etc., from chapter one to **support your predictions**.

THE GREAT GATSBY

6. What is your impression of Nick's neighbor, the one who reaches toward the green light across the water? Might this be a symbol for something? Without researching the green light and its meanings, what do you suppose its purpose may be for this mysterious man? What is *your* prediction?

THE GREAT GATSBY

Ch. 1: Post-Reading, Pre-Discussion Quiz   Name_____

1. ___ What college did Nick and Tom attend?

    A. Oxford
    B. New Haven
    C. Princeton
    D. Harvard

2. ___ What sport did Tom play in college?

    A. baseball
    B. fencing
    C. polo
    D. football

3. ___ Who lives next to Nick Carroway?

    A. Mr. Wolfsheim
    B. The Buchanans
    C. Jordan Baker
    D. Myrtle and Wilson
    E. Jay Gatsby

4. ___ Which words would best describe Tom Buchanan?

    A. Brutish and insensitive
    B. Gentlemanly and contented
    C. Understanding and tolerant
    D. Flirtatious and happy-go-lucky

5. ___ Which words best describe Daisy Buchanan?

    A. Relaxed and confident
    B. Flighty and a bit anxious
    C. Happy in her domestic situation
    D. A restless alcoholic

6. ___ Which words best describe Jordan Baker?

    A. Nervous and ambitious
    B. Drunk and lazy
    C. Sweet and pure
    D. Sophisticated and bored

THE GREAT GATSBY

7. ___Which words would best describe Jay Gatsby?

    A. Brutish and insensitive
    B. Athletic and down-to-earth
    C. Hopeful and striving
    D. Gentlemanly and contented

8. ___The main characters are living

    A. along Puget Sound
    B. in downtown New York City
    C. on Easter Egg Island
    D. along the Long Island Sound

THE GREAT GATSBY

CHAPTER ONE: Pre-Discussion Critical Summary for the Teacher

Concept: Characterization
Skills Practiced: Find passages that characterize major figures; draw conclusions.

Nick Carroway: Nick is the narrator, and Fitzgerald devotes considerable energy to earn the reader's trust in him. He comes across as curious and non-judgmental (His father taught him to be this way); and he has been privy to the confessions of all types of men because of his tolerance (although by the end of the novel, Nick will emerge unafraid to form judgments). Out of a sense of boredom and a related longing for adventure, Nick moves to the East to try his hand at finance in the big city. He finds a small house to rent in West Egg on Long Island next to a very large mansion. The story is told from his first person perspective. Because Nick is somewhat non-judgmental, this puts him in an excellent position to narrate the story relatively objectively. He's also not particularly close to his second cousin Daisy, so he's not as biased as he might otherwise be. He has impressions of each of the Buchanans from short-lived past experiences, and went to college (New Haven) with Daisy's husband.

Tom and Daisy Buchanan: Tom is clearly arrogant, bigoted, and a brute, as is apparent by his own statements about the races (12-13) and Daisy's physical and emotional marks of abuse (12). He was once a great football star, went to New Haven (Yale) with Nick, and is having an affair. Daisy's comments inform the reader that she is hurt by Tom's actions. How long the affair has persisted is not clear. But Daisy seems to understand her predicament as a confined and powerless woman of high society, and tells the story of her daughter's birth while "Tom was God knows where." When she discovered she had a baby girl, she cried and hoped that her daughter would grow up to be a "beautiful little fool" (16-17). Daisy is flighty, and she tries to put up a cheerful front, though she is clearly sad. But she becomes alert at the mention of the name "Gatsby." She appears to know him, though the reader does not know how, at this point.

Jordan Baker: Already, we see that Jordan promises to be a conduit of information for Nick. She is clearly a bored sophisticate and not apparently disturbed or surprised by the affair between Tom and this woman. She is amused by the drama brewing between her friends, Tom and Daisy (14-15). It is this amusement, and not the immorality of Tom's pursuits, that excites her. Her comportment will become increasingly important as the novel progresses.

Gatsby: Nick clearly thinks that Gatsby is an interesting person and full of Romantic hope (as in *Romanticism*). Gatsby stands on the dock and looks at the stars with the sort of gaze of the figure in the famous Romantic painting, **Wanderer Above the Sea of Fog, by Casper David Friedrich (1818).** Nick says he has a "heightened sensitivity to the promises of life" and "There was something gorgeous about him" (2). Gatsby is a mysterious figure in these early stages of the book, as he stretches his hand across the

Sound toward the green light. We don't meet him in person until the novel (and the gossip) is well underway.

THE GREAT GATSBY

Scene from Chapter 1   *At the "Tom Buchanans"*

DIRECTIONS: In a group of four, read the following script, adapted from chapter one of *The Great Gatsby*. Then, for the character whose part you played, complete the characterization chart with the other classmates who also read your part in their own reading groups (i.e. Nick or Tom or Daisy or Jordan).

Setting: Nick has just met with Tom Buchanan outside of his mansion. The two are now walking inside to meet with Daisy. "The only completely stationary object in the room was an enormous couch on which two young women were buoyed up as though upon an anchored balloon. . . . The younger of the two was a stranger to [Nick]. She was extended full length at her end of the divan, completely motionless, and with her chin raised a little, as if she were balancing something on it which was quite likely to fall." Daisy is reclined on the other side.

Daisy *(leaning slightly forward and with an absurd, charming little laugh, and drawing her delicate hand out to Nick, who takes her hand and kisses it)* I'm p-paralyzed with happiness.

Nick *(laughing)*: I stopped off in Chicago for a day on my way East. A dozen people send their love.

Daisy: Do they miss me?

Nick: *(teasing her warmly and affectionately)* The whole town is desolate. All the cars have the left rear wheel painted black as a mourning wreath, and there's a persistent wail all night along the north shore.

Daisy: *(laughing again)* How gorgeous! Let's go back, Tom. To-morrow! *(adding irreverently)* You ought to see the baby.

Nick: I'd like to.

Daisy: She's asleep. She's three years old. Haven't you ever seen her?

Nick: Never

Daisy: Well, you ought to see her. She's—

Tom *(resting his hand upon Nick's shoulder)*: What you doing, Nick?

Nick: I'm a bond man.

Tom: Who with?

THE GREAT GATSBY

Nick: Miller and Gross

Tom: *(decisively)* Never heard of them.

Nick: *(annoyed by Tom's tone of voice)* You will. You will if you stay in the East.

Tom: Oh, I'll stay in the East, don't you worry *(glancing at Daisy)*. I'd be a God damned fool to live anywhere else.

Jordan: Absolutely! *(Jordan then yawns elegantly and stands up)* I'm stiff. I've been lying on that sofa for as long as I can remember.

Daisy: Don't look at me. I've been trying to get you to New York all afternoon.
The butler shows Jordan a tray of cocktails.

Jordan: *(to the cocktails being offered)* No thanks. I'm absolutely in training.

Tom: *(looking at her incredulously)* You are! How you ever get anything done is beyond me.

Jordan: *(to Nick, a little dryly)* You live in West Egg. I know somebody there. You must know Gatsby.

Daisy: *(alarmed and demanding)* Gatsby? What Gatsby?

Butler: Dinner is served. *The four walk to the dinner table outside.*

Daisy: *(disgusted)* Why candles? *(She snaps them all out with her fingers)* In two weeks it'll be the longest day in the year. *(smiling radiantly at the rest of the group)* Do you always watch for the longest day of the year and then miss it? I always watch for the longest day in the year and then miss it.

Jordan: *(bored)* We ought to plan something.

Daisy: All right, what'll we plan? *(turning quickly to Nick, sounding helpless)* What do people plan? *(suddenly, Daisy looks with awe at her little finger)* Look! I hurt it. You did it, Tom *(she says this accusingly)*. I know you didn't mean to, but you *did* do it. That's what I get for marrying a brute of a man, a great, big, hulking physical specimen of a---

Tom: *(interrupting crossly)* I hate that word hulking, even in kidding.

Daisy: *(insistently)* Hulking. *They drink and eat.*

19

THE GREAT GATSBY

Nick: You make me feel uncivilized, Daisy. Can't you talk about crops or something?

Tom: *(violently and out of nowhere)* Civilization has gone to pieces . I've gotten to be a terrible pessimist about things. Have you read "The Rise of the Colored Empires" by this man Godard? Well, it's a fine book, and everybody ought to read it. The idea is if we don't look out the white race will be—will be utterly submerged. It's all scientific stuff; it's been proved.

Daisy: *(with an expression of unthoughtful sadness)* Tom's getting very profound. He reads deep books with long words in them. What was that word we—

Tom: *(glancing impatiently at Daisy)* Well, these books are all scientific. This fellow has worked out the whole thing. It's up to us, who are the dominant race, to watch out or these other races will have control of things.

Daisy: *(winking at Nick)* We've got to beat them down.

Jordan: You ought to live in California.

Tom: *(interrupting impatiently)* This idea is that we're Nordics. I am, and you are, and you are, and *(while he is saying this, Daisy winks at Nick again)* and *(looking briefly at Daisy)*. . . and we've produced all the things that go to make civilization—oh, science and art, and all that. Do you see?
A telephone rings from inside the house. The butler, who has been standing by, leaves the porch to answer it. Almost at the same time, Daisy leans into Nick . . . .

Daisy: I'll tell you a family secret *(whispering enthusiastically)*. It's about the butler's nose. Do you want to hear about the butler's nose?

Nick: *(with an ironic smile as if participating in a joke)* That's why I came over to-night.

Daisy: Well, he wasn't always a butler; he used to be the silver polisher for some people in New York that had a silver service for two hundred people. He had to polish it from morning till night, until finally it began to affect his nose—

Jordan: Things went from bad to worse.

Daisy: Yes. Things went from bad to worse, until finally he had to give up his position. *The butler comes back and whispers into Tom's ear, whereupon Tom frowns, pushes back his chair, and without a word goes inside. As if his absence quickens something within her, Daisy leans forward again, her voice glowing and singing.*

THE GREAT GATSBY

Daisy: I love to see you at my table, Nick. You remind me of a—of a rose, an absolute rose. *(turning to Jordan)* Doesn't he? An absolute rose?
Suddenly, Daisy throws her napkin on the table and excuses herself and goes into the house.

Nick: (*a little awkwardly*) So, you

Jordan: Sh! *(Jordan leans forward, trying to hear what's going on in the house)*

Nick: This Mr. Gatsby you spoke of is my neighbor—

Jordan: *(smiling)* Don't talk. I want to hear what happens.

Nick: *(innocently)* Is something happening?

Jordan: *(surprised)* You mean to say you don't know? I thought everybody knew.

Nick: I don't.

Jordan: (*leaning forward a little hesitantly*) Why—Tom's got some woman in New York.

Nick: (*blankly*) Got some woman? *Jordan nods in the affirmative.*

Jordan: She might have the decency not to telephone him at dinner time. Don't you think? *Before Nick can say anything, Tom and Daisy come back to the table.*

Daisy: (*with tense and embarrassed gayety*) It couldn't be helped!
Daisy sits back down and glances searchingly at Jordan and then at Nick and continues . . . . I looked outdoors for a minute and it's very romantic outdoors. There's a bird on the lawn that I think must be a nightingale come over on the Cunard or White Star Line. He's singing away. (*she sings a little*). It's romantic, isn't it Tom?

Tom: (*miserably to Nick*) Very romantic. (*leaning in to Nick*) If it's light enough after dinner, I want to take you down to the stables.
There is some discussion (to be extemporized), and then Tom and Jordan stroll into the house. Nick and Daisy walk around the garden a bit and then sit down. Suddenly, Daisy takes her face in her hands as if feeling its lovely shape, and her eyes gradually out into the velvet dusk. Turbulent emotions begin to possess her, which he keeps a little subdued.

Daisy: We don't know each other very well, Nick. Even if we are cousins. You didn't come to my wedding.

Nick: I wasn't back from the war.

THE GREAT GATSBY

Daisy: That's true. . . . Well, I've had a very bad time, Nick, and I'm pretty cynical about everything. *There is an awkward pause, and then Nick says, trying to lighten things up,*

Nick: (*referring to her daughter*) I suppose she talks, and—eats, and everything.

Daisy: (*absently*) Oh, yes. . . . Listen, Nick; let me tell you what I said when she was born. Would you like to hear?

Nick: Very much.

Daisy: It'll show you how I've gotten to feel about—things. Well, she was less than an hour old and Tom was God knows where. I woke up out of the ether with an utterly abandoned feeling, and asked the nurse right away if it was a boy or a girl. She told me it was a girl, and so I turned my head away and wept. (*with great emotion and defiantly*) All right, I said, I'm glad it's a girl. And I hope she'll be a fool—that's the best thing a girl can be in this world, a beautiful little fool. . . . You see I think everything's terrible anyhow. Everybody thinks so—the most advanced people. And I *know*. I've been everywhere and seen everything and done everything. (*Her eyes are defiant and then she laughs with a thrilling scorn*) . Sophisticated—God, I'm sophisticated!

THE GREAT GATSBY

CHARACTERIZATION WORKSHEET Your Name _____

Full Name of Assigned Character: _____

Background and Relationship to other Characters (friend of, husband of, etc.) :

What this character looks like, says and does:

What the narrator says about this character:

What other characters communicate about this character through speech and action:

Based on your findings, write a short character description of this character. Include two or three short quotes in the body of your description. Use a separate sheet of paper.

THE GREAT GATSBY

Ch. 1: Post-Discussion QUEST   Name_____

DIRECTIONS: Choose the sentence that corresponds to the correct vocabulary word:

1. ____Extemporizing   A. The boys had fun ___ over their favorite, rival teams.

2. ____Supercilious   B. The plaintiff looked ___ at the defendant in court.

3. ____Fractiousness   C. She forgot her notes, so she relied upon ___.

4. ____Contemptuously   D. After winning the award, she behaved in a ___ manner.

5. ____Bantering   E. She had to use a harness to control the dog's ___.

DIRECTIONS: Respond to the following on a separate sheet of paper:

1. Describe TWO of the following characters, drawing upon the methods of *characterization*. (Jordan, Nick, Tom, Daisy). Use complete sentences and your best formal writing.

THE GREAT GATSBY

Chapter Two

Pre-Reading Journal Question:

- Is it ever okay to cheat on a romantic partner or spouse? Can you think of an instance in which it may be forgivable that a person strikes up an intense relationship with a person other than the partner or spouse? Explain your reasoning.

Vocabulary Review: In chapter two, you will encounter the following words. For each word, find its definition and write a sentence using the word correctly. Be sure there is enough information in your sentence so your teacher can tell that you understand *how* the word is used. **Do not simply repeat the word's definition in your sentence.** Identify its part of speech as written below (i.e., adjective, noun, verb, adverb):

- Solemn
- Contiguous
- Sensuously
- Vigorously
- Deft
- Imagery (literary term)
- Setting (literary term)

Preview of Class Discussion:

1. Make a list of all of the places mentioned in chapter two, focusing especially upon those which the narrator spends a good deal of time describing. Add to each a list of words and phrases the narrator uses to describe these places. Pay attention to **imagery**.

2. Based upon your collection of words and phrases, how would you **interpret** these places? How do they provide a fitting backdrop for the characters that abide there (compare the characters to the world in which they live)? How do they provide a fitting backdrop for the characters just passing through or visiting (compare and contrast)?

3. Describe Myrtle and George Wilson, separately and as a couple. How would you evaluate their relationship? What, do you assume, is at the heart of Myrtle's treatment of her husband? Find phrases from the chapter that support your **assumptions**.

4. What more do you learn about Tom? How does this affect your view of him? Is there anything you find sympathetic about him? What do you think are his motivations for his actions as described in chapter two? Is he without excuse?

THE GREAT GATSBY

Ch. 2: Post-Reading, <u>Pre-Discussion</u> Quiz   Name_____

1. ___Nick meets all of the following persons at Tom's New York apartment, **EXCEPT**
    a. An effeminate photographer
    b. Catherine, a woman of about thirty
    c. Mary Pickford, the silent screen actress

2. ___<u>According to Myrtle's sister</u>, why doesn't Tom divorce Daisy and marry Myrtle?
    a. Because Daisy is Catholic and she doesn't believe in divorce.
    b. Because Myrtle does not want to hurt her husband.
    c. Because Tom wants to break the news to Daisy gently.

3. ___Which profession is associated with the billboard looming over the Valley of Ashes?
    a. Law
    b. Insurance
    c. Optometry

4. ___What does Tom purchase for Myrtle while in NYC?
    a. A diamond necklace
    b. A dog
    c. A book
    d. Tickets to a Broadway Show

5. ___The Valley of Ashes can be described as
    a. Cheerful and inviting
    b. Stark and alienating
    c. Romantic and charming
    d. Bustling with the excitement of life

6. ___Which words <u>best</u> describe Myrtle?
    a. Ladylike and sophisticated
    b. Educated and intelligent
    c. Nurturing and domestic
    d. Lively and class conscious

7. ___What words best describe Myrtle's husband, George Wilson?
    a. Successful and energetic
    b. Weak and ineffectual
    c. Strong and decisive

THE GREAT GATSBY

CHAPTER TWO: Pre-Discussion Critical Summary for the Teacher

Concepts: Multisensory Imagery, setting

Reading Skill: Interpreting the effect of multisensory imagery associated with a setting or backdrop for characters in a story.

The **imagery** is interesting and provocative in this chapter. The valley of ashes takes the forms of men who "move dimly" and houses that are "already crumbling". Adverbs and adjectives used are bleak: dimly, crumbling, ghastly, impenetrable, leaden, foul, dismal . . . perhaps like **T.S. Eliot's "The Wasteland"** imagery (23-4). (Eliot's poem appeared just three years before *The Great Gatsby*.)

The first recognizable **symbol** is Doctor T.J. Eckleburg, a billboard at the Valley of Ashes. It is an advertisement for an optometrist who is probably out of business. There is no face, just eyes that brood on over the solemn dumping ground. One critic linked Doctor Eckleburg to Nick Carroway, an interesting comparison, because both are rather objective viewers of the novel's action. Later, Wilson likens the advertisement to God's own eyes, which see everything and will bring everything to light. But like the faded billboard, God seems to be a faded memory for a large majority of the inhabitants of 1920s New York City, where the morals seem loose, and whose absence will become apparent in relationship to people like George Wilson, whose God certainly does not help him to flourish.

Myrtle Wilson, Tom's "girl": She behaves in a silly, scandal loving, mutable, and playful way, except concerning the subject of Daisy Buchanan. The reader may sense at this point that she is having an affair with Tom because she is a social climber and not satisfied with her own husband and life style. Clearly, the greater context is one in which the cult of celebrity is in full swing, much like our own age. For the first time in United States history, girls want to be like fashionable celluloid goddesses. Myrtle is no different (27). She believes Tom can give her the life she wants; he keeps her interested by buying her the clothes and presents she'd never be able to afford through her husband. In Myrtle's eyes, Tom's ever-present example throws the constant flares of unfavorable light upon George Wilson. While Daisy relaxes coolly in their East Egg mansion, Myrtle boils away in an apartment above Wilson's Garage. However, Myrtle is not attuned to the kind of husband Tom is for Daisy, who is also frustrated with her own marriage, but for different reasons. In Tom, Myrtle sees strength and power; in her husband, she sees flaccid ineptitude.

Wilson: He is Myrtle's husband. He runs the gas station across from the billboard, and is described as spiritless, anemic, and pale (25). Things are not going well for him financially, though he is making an honest living running his own business. His wife is unkind toward and impatient with him. She walks through him as if he were a ghost, orders him to get some chairs, and says to his face that she made a mistake in marrying him. There are always those places, those neighborhoods, kept hidden from tourists. In Fitzgerald's New York and Long Island, the Valley of Ashes is the valley of the wasted, of the discarded, perhaps of discarded dreams and the shells of human beings who have been trampled by those in a state of thoughtless privilege or entitlement. The fates of Mr. and Mrs. Wilson will further solidify this view.

Events: Tom breaks Myrtle's nose with his open hand when she repeats Daisy's name loudly in a jealous rage (37). Tom is lying to Myrtle about his plans to leave Daisy; however, he is just having a good time with no intentions of leaving his wife (33).

THE GREAT GATSBY

Drawing Project: *Imagery* **in Chapter Two**

The description of the Valley of Ashes in chapter two is extremely important to your understanding and interpretation of the novel. For *at least* this reason, the author spends much time working out the detailed imagery associated with the valley. In order to help you come to a more intimate understanding of this important place, create a picture of the valley that is accurate to its description in the novel. You may add your own artistic flare, of course, but your picture needs to demonstrate careful reading.

Before you begin, collect a list of multi-sensory imagery descriptions and plans for your picture.

THE GREAT GATSBY

Ch. 2: Post-Discussion QUEST   Name_____

Choose the correct synonyms for each of the following vocabulary words:

___ 1. Solemn   A. Strongly; actively; energetically

___ 2. Contiguous   B. Skillful; Expert; adept

___ 3. Sensuously   C. Attached; connecting; adjoining

___ 4. Vigorously   D. Serious; somber; grave

___ 5. Deft   E. Sensing; sexually; gratifyingly

DIRECTIONS: Answer the following questions on a separate sheet of paper:

- How has your impression of Tom Buchanan grown or changed after reading chapter two? Explain.

- What is the point of the elaborate description of the Valley of Ashes? How does the author use imagery to communicate his point? Use quotes/examples from the passage and discuss them. Use complete sentences and your best formal writing. Add pages as needed.

THE GREAT GATSBY

Chapter Three

Pre-Reading Journal Questions: Choose one:

1. Have you ever participated in or been the victim of gossip? Explain. What are the effects of gossip?
2. Have you ever cheated in order to win a game, get a good grade on a quiz/test, or on anything else? If so, why do you think you did it? Why do people cheat?

Vocabulary Review: In chapter three, you will encounter the following words. For each word, find its definition and write a sentence using the word correctly. Be sure there is enough information in your sentence so your teacher can tell that you understand *how* the word is used. **Do not simply repeat the meaning of your word in the sentence.** Identify its part of speech as written below (i.e., adjective, noun, verb, adverb):

- Permeate
- Innuendo
- Prodigality
- Vehemently
- Credulity
- Homogeneity
- Staid
- Impetuously
- Notorious
- Vacuous
- Florid
- Corpulent
- Malevolence
- Poignant

Preview of Class Discussion:

1. What types of people come to Gatsby's parties? How well do they know Gatsby?

2. In chapter 3, there is a description of a chorus girl singing. Reread the entire passage, picturing the details of her performance in your mind. What is the author's **intended effect** of this passage **upon the reader**?

3. What are people saying about Gatsby?

4. What, do *you* think, are the reasons for including so much **detail** about the preparations for the party and the various people who attend the party? How

THE GREAT GATSBY

might these details affect how you see Gatsby? How do these details affect how you see the party guests?

5. Why is Nick so surprised to find that his conversation with a stranger is actually a conversation with Gatsby, himself? Shouldn't he at least know what his host looks like?

6. Why do you think the party ends with the car crash involving the owl-eyed man (Owl Eyes)?

7. What does Nick decide is behind Jordan's "bored haughty face"?

8. What more do you learn about Jordan? What could be the reason she says to Nick, "I hate careless people. That's why I like you"? Do you believe her?

9. What does Nick say about who is honest and who is not? Do you believe him? Why or why not?

10. Why do you think Fitzgerald suspends our first meeting with Gatsby until chapter three?

THE GREAT GATSBY

Ch. 3: Post-Reading, Pre-Discussion Quiz   Name_____

1. ___Gatsby's party includes all of the following, **EXCEPT**
   - A. Orange and Lemon juices
   - B. An orchestra
   - C. Uninvited guests
   - D. A Christmas tree

2. ___How was Nick invited to the party?
   - A. Gatsby saw him on the lawn and invited him.
   - B. Gatsby telephoned him with an informal invitation.
   - C. The chauffeur presented him with a formal invitation.
   - D. Nick just wandered into the party out of curiosity.

3. ___At the party, Nick runs into
   - A. Tom Buchanan
   - B. Daisy Buchanan
   - C. Myrtle Wilson
   - D. None of the Above

4. ___At the party, Lucille says, "When I was here last I tore my gown on a chair, and **he** asked me my name and address—inside of a week I got a package from Croirier's with a new evening gown in it." *Who is **he**?*
   - A. Mr. Mumble
   - B. Tom Buchanan
   - C. Jay Gatsby
   - D. The chauffeur

5. ___All of the following gossipy tales are told about Gatsby (at the party), **EXCEPT**
   - A. He killed a man once.
   - B. He fixed the 1919 World Series
   - C. He was a German spy during the war.
   - D. All of the above was said about Gatsby.

6. ___Gatsby often calls Nick
   - A. Old Sport
   - B. Old Friend
   - C. Old Buddy
   - D. Neighbor

7. ___In chapter 3, Gatsby's manner towards Nick can be BEST described as
   - A. Sinister and Menacing
   - B. Playful and Exciting
   - C. Flirtatious and Animated

D. Reassuring and Understated

8. ___ Why is Owl Eyes so astonished by Gatsby's library?
   A. It is the largest of all the libraries he's ever seen.
   B. Because the books on the shelf are real books, not fake.
   C. Because the bookcases are about 30-feet high.
   D. Because it looks like a Gothic cathedral.

9. ___ We find out that Jordan likely cheated in which one of the following?
   A. Golf
   B. Poker
   C. Dating
   D. Her college exam

10. ___ Chapter three ends with a car crash. What familiar person was "not even trying" to drive the car?
    A. Owl Eyes
    B. Klipspringer
    C. Jordan
    D. Gatsby

THE GREAT GATSBY

CHAPTER THREE: Pre-Discussion Critical Summary for the Teacher
Reading Skills Practiced: Identifying the intended effect, interpreting the effect of details, reading pictures as text.

Chapter three begins with preparations for Gatsby's party. Gatsby is still personally unknown to Nick, but Gatsby extends him a written invitation to attend the party. Most people, on the other hand, come uninvited, and are bussed out in style from the city, retrieved from the train station by chauffers, or else drive themselves, arriving early in the day to swim and loiter on the beach, and staying well past midnight until the drunken reveries begin to fade or sour. It is a layered chapter, filled with multiple scene descriptions, conversations, and variations in tone. It contains everything from highly humorous accounts of histrionic singers and drunken innuendo to human mishaps and insightful commentary. The chapter should, of course, be read with attention to the author's felicitous phrasing. For example, he describes the evening at Gatsby's as if it was a suspended star lighting the universe above the Earth's darkening rotation: "the lights grow brighter as the earth lurches away from the sun, and now the orchestra is playing yellow cocktail music. . . . Laughter is easier minute by minute, spilled with prodigality tripped out at a cheerful word" (40).

Before Nick slinks away in solitude through the convivial clusters of conversation, Jordan arrives, saving Nick from total isolation. She has a date, but spends much of her time talking to Nick throughout the evening. In their wanderings and throughout the "first supper" (an intriguing allusion to Christ's last supper?), Nick gains a very sinister and intriguing view of Gatsby, the man who throws uproarious parties, but whose face is never recognized, even when he attends. Some say "he killed a man once." Another claims he was "a German spy during the war" (44). Nick and Jordan attempt to ferret out the host from hiding, but Gatsby remains elusive. While on their reconnaissance, she and Nick step into a Gothic library where sits Owl Eyes, wide-eyed with astonishment because the bookshelves hold real, solid books and not just their facades. Apparently, this is his proof of Gatsby's authenticity, and an indication of the real possibility that many people owned the look of a library but never the actual library. This cannot be an arbitrary detail, as *The Great Gatsby* is largely a meditation on the **real versus the unreal**, of **truth and deception**. Although Gatsby, himself, can command the greatest show on Earth, Owl Eyes's discovery tempts us to take Gatsby for the real thing, whatever that "thing" turns out to be (45-6).

After an unsuccessful search for the host, Nick finds through conversation that Gatsby is sitting right across from him (47). Both men are surprised and embarrassed, Nick for not recognizing his gracious host, and Gatsby for not being accessible enough to be recognized by his guest. Gatsby turns out to be nothing like what Nick expected: "I had expected that Mr. Gatsby would be a florid and corpulent person in his middle years." By contrast, Gatsby is young, elegant, and attractive, although a little "roughnecked." He is gracious, understated, and consistently sober. Nick's evocative description of Gatsby's smile reveals its poetry:

> It was one of those rare smiles with a quality of eternal reassurance in it, that you may come across four or five times in life. It faced—or seemed to face—the whole external world for an instant, and then concentrated on *you* with an irresistible prejudice in your favor. It understood you just as far as you wanted to be understood, believed in you as you would like to believe in yourself, and assured you that it had precisely the impression of you that, at your best, you hoped to convey. Precisely at that point it vanished—and I was looking at an elegant young roughneck, a year or two over thirty, whose elaborate formality of speech just missed being absurd. (48)

Later, Gatsby has Jordan summoned for an hour-long meeting. Afterwards, Jordan tells Nick only that "It was . . . simply amazing. . . . But I swore I wouldn't tell it and here I am tantalizing you." Now, the reader, too, is tantalized (52).

Chapter three also presents a good opportunity to work with some **United States History**, **cartography**, and **primary sources**, including World War I, jazz music, the economic climate in the 1920s (reflecting financial opportunities for success and failure—Nick is a "bondsman" or a financer), old maps of New York City, automobiles of 1922, visual depictions of NYC street scenes (photographs, film, painting), as well as old advertisements of such items as cigarettes. What a great opportunity (for the AP student, especially) to practice **reading pictures** and other visual primary sources **as texts**. See the class activity for this chapter on the next pages.

The Theme of Recklessness: Chapter three also develops the character of Jordan, and her depiction is not a flattering one. She is cordial enough, but her indifference and haughty face are outward expressions of her dishonesty and carelessness. She very likely cheats at golf and thoughtlessly puts pedestrians and others in danger. When Nick admonishes her for driving her car "so close to some workmen that our fender flicked a button on one man's coat," she is flippant: "They'll keep out of my way. . . . It takes two to make an accident" (57-8). The real danger, it would appear, is not in the tales of Gatsby's sinister dealings with a fantastic devil, but in the consequences of this sort of recurring demonstration of indifference toward the feelings and welfare of others (others like George and Myrtle). Nick's commentary on Jordan is an extension of the party's culminating event, a hilariously described **car accident**, in which Owl Eyes and a "pale, dangling individual" attempt to drive home drunk and run into a wall, "amputating" the front wheel (54-5). There are both specific and broad correlations between this very funny accident and the very serious one in chapter seven, and both highlight the theme of careless recklessness inherent in the actions of Jordan Baker, Tom, and Daisy. Similarly, some critics have drawn connections between this scene and **The Crash of 1929**, as well as Gatsby's own downfall.

THE GREAT GATSBY

Reading Images: Teacher-Led Class Activity followed by Individual Practice

A great activity for follow-up to chapter three is to teach/review with the students how to interpret an image (You can use the direct instruction method, or work through an example in its entirety before asking the students to experience the interpretive process on their own). There are plenty of now historic places, advertisements and scenes mentioned in *The Great Gatsby* to give you search terms for a regular Google Image Search. Nonetheless, I have listed some reputable sites with which students should become familiar in accessing legitimate primary sources. Just type in the approximate dates and/or places of interest and see what surfaces. The **sixth** link is from AP Central and is a review of how to read an image with or without an accompanying text.

Possible images connected to *The Great Gatsby,* so far:

- Murray Hill Hotel
- Pennsylvania Station
- World War I photographs
- New York City street scene (1920s, of course)
- Fifth Avenue
- Long Island
- Central Park
- Queens
- Advertisements (1920s—cigarettes, businesses, cars, home appliances)

Links:
1. http://www.digitalhistory.uh.edu   Digital History
2. http://www.loc.gov   Library of Congress
3. http://www.smithsonianmag.com/   Smithsonian Magazine
4. http://www.eyewitnesstohistory.com/index.html   Eyewitness to History
5. http://www.shmoop.com/1920s/   Shmoop (Look for images/photos)
6. http://apcentral.collegeboard.com/apc/members/courses/teachers_corner/158521.html   Reading Images: An Approach and Demonstration

On the next page are the four interpretive steps, as outlined by Robert DiYanni.
I now use for my example the image called, "Migrant Mother", the famous photograph taken by Annie Lebowitz. I use this classic, historic photograph as my example because it has worked so well for me in the past. However, you may want to work solely with an image from the 1920s to introduce the concept. In any case, I would insist that the students work with images from the 1920s. The four steps are not always mutually exclusive, but students should not miss the initial step of collecting all the details.

THE GREAT GATSBY

How to Read an Image

1. **Make observations**: Without interpreting, just say aloud or write down what it is that you see. Try to notice everything. Say aloud, for example, "I see a woman." "I see a baby." . . . "I see dirt on a boy's face." . . . . "I see a tent." . . . .

2. **Connect the observations**: Make comparisons between the disparate parts of the image you have noticed; Notice contrasts between each detail, as well. For example: "Both the mother and the children are frowning." "The boy is burying his face in the mother, while the other child is standing." "They are all in a tent of some kind." . . . . "The photo is called 'Migrant Mother.'". . .

3. **Draw inferences from the related observations**: Based upon your observations and their connections to each other, decide what you can conclude about the picture. For example, I might say "The woman in the picture is the mother of the children in the picture." . . . "The mother and her children are living in a tent." . . . "There is no father pictured in the photo." . . . "Based upon the title of the picture, they are living as a migrant family." . . . "The father is probably away working." . . . "They are all dressed in clothes that do not pertain to our own age, so I would guess the photograph was taken in the 1930s or 40s."

4. **Formulate a tentative interpretive conclusion**: This is where you would forward your interpretation, based upon your observations, connections, and inferences. For example, I might conclude the following:

   > The mother does not just look unhappy, she looks worried and perhaps appears older than what is true. The father is away working, while the mother is home at the tent taking care of the children. They are all probably hungry. The mother is likely worried about whether she'll be able to continue to feed herself and her children. The title, "Migrant Mother" tells us they are a migrant family with nowhere else to go. Migrant workers in California were prevalent during the Depression, so this is probably the Depression Era of the 1930s. They have very likely fled the Dust Bowl with other migrant families, as the migration of Dust Bowl families to California occurred after several devastating dust storms in the 1930s. The woman (mother) appears to be of Native American descent, possibly Cherokee, which may place the family as coming from Oklahoma, or the Texas Panhandle, both ravaged by the 1930s dust storms. Oklahoma is well known for its large Native American population, due to the earlier mandates of Jackson's Indian Removal Act, which pushed several Native American tribes, especially the Cherokee, from the Southeastern United States into Oklahoma.

THE GREAT GATSBY

Ch. 3: Post-Discussion QUEST Name_____

Place each of the following words in their correct sentence below. Four words will NOT be used:

- A. Permeate
- B. Innuendo
- C. Prodigality
- D. Vehemently
- E. Credulity
- F. Homogeneity
- G. Staid
- H. Impetuously
- I. Notorious
- J. Vacuous
- K. Florid
- L. Corpulent
- M. Malevolence
- N. Poignant

Al Capone was a (1) _____ gangster and the *alleged* mastermind behind the St. Valentine's Day Massacre in Chicago, 1929. This was never proved, and the police were only able to arrest him for tax evasion two years later.

The dogs broke into the pantry and ate all the cookies (2) _____.

The villain grinned with a horrible look of absolute (3) _____.

Her fever made her face (4) _____.

I felt (5) _____ after eating a whole pizza by myself.

The graduation speech was deep, well articulated and (6) _____.

The spices will (7) _____ the broth, but only if you let the soup simmer for a while.

The pastor preached (8) _____ against abortion.

She was speechless in front of the audience; she just stood there with a (9) _____ look in her eyes.

While watching Houdini in a state of absolute (10) _____, she fully believed that all of the magician's tricks were performed with the use of real magic.

THE GREAT GATSBY

11. In chapter 3, there is a description of a chorus girl:

> One of the girls in yellow was playing the piano, and beside her stood a tall, red-haired young lady from a famous chorus, engaged in song. She had drunk a quantity of champagne, and during the course of her song she had decided, ineptly, that everything was very, very sad—she was not only singing, she was weeping too. Whenever there was a pause in the song she filled it with gasping, broken sobs, and then took up the lyric again in a quavering soprano. The tears coursed down her cheeks—not freely, however, for when they came into contact with her heavily beaded eyelashes they assumed an inky color, and pursued the rest of their way in slow black rivulets. A humorous suggestion was made that she sing the notes on her face, whereupon she threw up her hands, sank into a chair, and went off into a deep vinous [wine induced] sleep.

_____ The narrator's INTENDED effect of this passage **upon the *reader*** is most likely:
   A. Melancholy and depression
   B. Pity and emotion
   C. Humor and mild curiosity
   D. Disgust and moral indignation

12. _____ The <u>two dashes</u> in the following passage below about Jordan <u>are most likely used for what purpose</u>?

> There was something more. I wasn't actually in love, but I felt a sort of tender curiosity. The bored haughty face that she turned to the world concealed something—most affectations conceal something eventually, even though they don't in the beginning—and one day I found what it was. (57)

   A. To prepare for a list.
   B. To signal a dramatic shift in tone.
   C. To set off commentary that deserves emphasis.
   D. All of the above.

13. _____ In the passage above (in #12), Nick says that Jordan's "bored haughty face" concealed something. What, according to the final paragraphs of the chapter, did it conceal?

   A. That she was a careless driver.
   B. That she was incurably dishonest.
   C. That she was, at bottom, very sad and lonely.
   D. That she was in all actuality slow witted.

THE GREAT GATSBY

14. _____ In referring to himself, Nick says
    A. I am one of the few honest people that I have ever known.
    B. I finally met someone who is just as careless as myself.
    C. I am the reckless type.
    D. I am not the type to frequent large parties.

DIRECTIONS: Answer the following question on a separate sheet of paper:

15. Chapter three does not develop very significantly any of the main characters we have come to know (with the slight exception of Jordan). Rather, it spends much time talking about Gatsby's guests and their trivial actions and conversations. However, the chapter itself is not trivial, for it is doing some important work. What is the likely significance or function of chapter three in the context of the novel?

THE GREAT GATSBY

Chapter Four: *The Great Gatsby*

Pre-Reading Journal Questions: Choose from the following:

1. Have you ever known anyone who is completely different from what you thought before you met or really knew him/her? Why do you think your initial impressions were so different from reality? Were you disappointed when you discovered that your first impressions were not real? Explain.
2. Have you ever lied about yourself in any *significant* ways? If so, then why did you do it? **OR**: Is it ever okay to tell lies about yourself? Explain.
3. What has been the most 'magical' event of your life, so far? Why do you think it was so magical?

Vocabulary Review: In chapter four, you will encounter most of the following words. For each word, find its definition and write a sentence using the word correctly. Be sure there is enough information in your sentence so your teacher can tell that you understand *how* the word is used. **Do not simply repeat the meaning of your word in the sentence.** Identify its part of speech as written below (i.e., adjective, noun, verb, adverb):

- Punctilious
- *In*credulity (the opposite of credulity)
- Somnambulatory (A form of 'somnambulate.')
- Benediction
- Denizen
- Juxtaposition
- Diction (a literary term you'll need for discussion and quizzes)
- Connotation (a rhetorical term)
- Setting (Look at its purpose in a literary work)
- Symbol (literary term)

Preview of Class Discussion:

1. Chapter four opens with the following sentence: "On Sunday morning while church bells rang in the villages alongshore, the world and its mistress returned to Gatsby's house and twinkled hilariously on his lawn." What is the author trying to convey with his word choice (**diction**) in phrases such as "the world and its mistress" and "twinkled hilariously". What is the **effect** of the **juxtaposition** (position of phrases near each other) between the villages alongshore and the world and its mistress?

2. Nick describes riding over the Queensboro Bridge. How is the bridge used as a **symbol?** A symbol for what? Why would Nick follow up with the sentence, "Even Gatsby could happen without any particular wonder"?

3. Who points out that his buttons are made of human molars? Why does he do this?

4. Meyer Wolfsheim tells Nick the story of Rosy Rosenthal and how he was shot outside the old Metropole, a restaurant "filled with faces dead and gone." As a follow-up to his recount of this event, Nick remembers that "Four of them [the gunmen] were electrocuted." Wolfsheim replies, "Five, with Becker" and then follows up with "I understand you're looking for a business gonnegtion." Nick's narration continues: "The juxtaposition of these two remarks was startling." **To which two remarks is he referring and why is the juxtaposition startling?**

5. Jordan and Gatsby, himself, provide new information about Gatsby's past. What new information do we learn and do you think the stories told by Jordan and Gatsby are believable? Why or why not?

6. Thus far in the novel, we have three well-described settings. These settings work to provide a backdrop for the characters dwelling there. They can very easily reflect these characters and their way of life, values, actions, and conflicts. See if you can find some correlations between the following settings and the characters that abide there:

    - East Egg: The Buchanans
    - West Egg: Gatsby and his patrons
    - The Valley of Ashes: The Wilsons
    - New York City: Wolfsheim, Tom and Myrtle together, the site of Nick's job

THE GREAT GATSBY

Ch. 4, Post-Reading, <u>Pre-Discussion</u> Quiz   Name_____

TRUE OR FALSE: Write out the ENTIRE word (i.e. *"True"* or *"False"*): If you are unsure about an answer, just write what you think is the correct answer and then follow it up with a brief, but clear explanation in the intervening space.

1. _____ Nick believes every detail of Gatsby's stories about his past.

2. _____ Gatsby shows Nick two items from his past: a picture of himself at Oxford and a medal of honor.

3. _____ Gatsby takes Nick to the old Metropole Restaurant; that is where he introduces Nick to Meyer Wolfsheim.

4. _____ While with Nick, Gatsby speaks, for a long time, to Tom Buchanan.

5. _____ Gatsby is in love with Jordan.

6. ___Whose cuff buttons are made of human molars?

    A. Jay Gatsby's
    B. Tom Buchanan's
    C. Meyer Wolfsheim's
    D. Rosy Rosenthal's

7. ___Mr. Wolfsheim is

    A. An actor
    B. A dentist
    C. A gambler
    D. A bootlegger

8. ___Who spots Daisy in a car (a white roadster) talking romantically with Gatsby?

    A. Tom
    B. Nick
    C. Jordan
    D. Myrtle

THE GREAT GATSBY

9. ___What was the catalyst to Daisy getting very drunk on the eve of her wedding day? Choose the best answer.

    A. She realized she hated the man she was about to marry.
    B. She had accidentally mixed two different drinks, and wasn't used to drinking.
    C. She lost the $350,000 string of pearls that Tom gave her.
    D. She had received a letter that threw her into emotional confusion.

10. ___Why did Gatsby buy the house (palace) in West Egg? (According to ch. 4 only)

    A. To be close to Daisy.
    B. To impress those who never believed in him.
    C. To rival or to spite Tom.
    D. Because it was his American dream to have a beautiful house and throw parties.

THE GREAT GATSBY

CHAPTER FOUR: Pre-Discussion Critical Summary for the Teacher

Literary Concepts: Juxtaposition, Setting, Diction, and Symbol

Reading Skill: Determining the meaning of a symbol, the purpose of word choices, and the effects of juxtaposition.

At the opening of chapter four, Nick offers a list of the people who attended Gatsby's parties all summer. He divides them, essentially, into two groups: East Eggers and West Eggers (62-3). The individuals from West Egg and NYC consist of those with new money (some with little money), the Irish, German, Italian, and Jewish immigrants, many from the film industry, Broadway, and others related, more or less, to famous capitalists, politicians and highly ranked officers of the American Legion. There is a contrast here between the old money families who tend to be more understated and feel more comfortable in their Oxford trousers, and the new money groups, who tend towards the entrepreneurial, the opportunistic, the ostentatious, and even the shady, for these groups must play the system to make their money, not simply inherit it. Of these guests, we meet Kipspringer, who apparently came to a Gatsby party and never left, taking advantage of gracious living for free. He is known to most as "the boarder." He will return to us later.

Now that Nick is more familiar with his landlord, Gatsby has grown a bit disappointing to him. How could he be otherwise after such a colossal build-up of rumors and glimpses of his romantic, **Übermensch (*Overman*) figure** at the end of the dock? Just knowing him now makes Gatsby seem much less intriguing, and this is a foretaste of Gatsby's dreams of Daisy shedding their magical nets in the next chapter. It is part of the **theme of disenchantment**. Gatsby, it seems to Nick, is not much of an illuminating talker, despite his illuminating smile, and there is clumsiness in his effort to be comfortable in elite company and to sport his expensive digs. He, too, is of West Egg; he has only lately acquired his fortune by his own stir, but the reader doesn't know this yet. For now, Gatsby would like everyone to believe the story he tells Nick on the way into the city (64-7).

Gatsby informs (not invites) Nick that he will be going to lunch with him. He intends to ask Nick for a favor, and wishes, in the meantime, to disabuse him of any unsavory notions concerning his character. But as we shall see, there is more to leave the reader believing than denying these rumors. He knows Nick must have heard at least some of them. But Gatsby's own story seems a bit far-fetched, as he relates the tale of his Oxford pedigree and heroic adventures in World War I. Furthermore, Gatsby says he's from "the Middle West," but when asked to specify, answers, "San Francisco" (65). Nonetheless, Gatsby provides Nick with some tangible proofs, such as the Medal of Honor from Montenegro and an old picture of himself among Oxford men in Trinity Quad.

THE GREAT GATSBY

Gatsby, too, is a fast driver, for he is stopped by a policeman who lets him go at the flash of a white card: "Right you are. . . . Know you next time, Mr. Gatsby. Excuse *me*!" (68). We discover that Gatsby did a favor for the commissioner. This is typical of the 1920s when, for instance, some police were paid off to allow entertainment establishments and gangsters to sell illegal alcohol. The students shouldn't know, definitively, that Gatsby is a bootlegger, *yet,* but the clues are adding up fast, especially in chapter four.

Next, we encounter an extended metaphor as the two men pass over the Queensboro Bridge (68-9), the bridge connecting Queens and Manhattan. The bridge is a thrilling symbol of the opening up of possibilities at its crossing into the big city, where everything and "anything can happen." In the queen of American cities, New York is a standing refutation of the morally conservative and the conventional; it eschews the rules and codes of conduct common to Nick's (and Gatsby's) "Middle West." What Nick notices is the complete opposite of the expected. In Nick's time, it was unheard of to see a limousine with African American patrons and a white chauffeur. The description leaves today's reader uncomfortable for its choice of words; however, for Nick, whose visits to the city in 1922 are still very fresh, it must have felt like a reversal of the natural order of the universe. And Gatsby is part of that reversal: "Anything can happen now that we've slid over this bridge . . . anything at all. . . . Even Gatsby could happen without any particular wonder."

While in town, Gatsby and Nick meet with Myer Wolfsheim (69-73) and their interactions give the reader more insight into what has possibly made Gatsby so wealthy. He is clearly caught up in an underworld related to gambling, possibly even gangster activity. He does business with Wolfsheim, the big shot gambler who fixed the 1919 World Series "with the single-mindedness of a burglar blowing a safe." Wolfsheim's sentimental reminiscence of his friend's (Rosy Rosenthal) murder at the old Metropole Restaurant solidifies our suspicions that he is tied to gangster activity. Wolfsheim seems emotional, but almost as soon as he says "they shot him three times in his full belly and drove away," he turns to Nick: "I understand you're looking for a business gonnegtion." This is a chilling shift, as Nick confesses: "The juxtaposition of these two remarks was startling" (70-1).

One final detail worth discussing are Wolfsheim's human molar cuff buttons, of which he is clearly proud: "Finest specimens of human molars" (72). It is a brilliant move on the part of the author to include both the molars and Wolfsheim's proud remark, because, though one can jettison a tooth with no real harm, it adds to the picture of a shady underworld, where a human being is a means to an end, where he can be hunted like an animal and whose more enduring physical parts can be commodified into little trophies. But, as we shall see, people like George and Myrtle Wilson are as disregarded as any animal. At the end of their lunch, Nick runs into Tom and attempts to engage Gatsby, but Gatsby is gone (74). The reader wonders why.

THE GREAT GATSBY

Finally, Nick meets Jordan at the Plaza Hotel tea garden that same afternoon, and he is astonished when he finally hears Gatsby's request. After all of the secrecy and the startling interactions with Gatsby's "gonnegtion", Nick finds humor in the modesty of Gatsby's request, that he wants Nick to invite Daisy to his house for tea, where Gatsby will show up. To provide context, Jordan tells Nick the story of Gatsby and Daisy's love affair back in Louisville, Kentucky in 1917, when she was only eighteen and he a young officer stationed there temporarily (74-7). Daisy was utterly enamored with Gatsby, or else exceedingly flattered by his romantic and endearing attentions. But his imminent departure for the war caused Daisy to pack her bags to see him off at the New York coastline. Her mother discovered her plan and grounded her, forbidding her ever to date another officer.

In a year's time, Daisy became engaged to "Tom Buchanan of Chicago." However, on the eve of her wedding day, Daisy received a letter (almost certainly from Gatsby) that threw her into emotional upheavals and sunk her into a drunken stupor. As Daisy had never been a drinker, the shock of the letter must have affected her in a very real and disturbing way (75-6). She made a decision to call off the marriage, but Jordan and the maid sobered her up in a cold bath. The next day, she married Tom without a hint of emotional disturbance. Four months later, Daisy seemed to have transferred all of her affections from Gatsby to Tom, for Jordan says she seemed exceedingly happy with him, and he with her. There is one difference: Tom was already having the first of a presumably long line of love affairs with working class women. Jordan tells Nick, "A week after I left Santa Barbara Tom ran into a wagon on the Ventura road one night, and ripped a front wheel off his car. The girl who was with him got into the papers, too, because her arm was broken—she was one of the chambermaids in the Santa Barbara Hotel" (77).

At last, much of the factual mystery behind Gatsby has now been disclosed: Gatsby bought the house on West Egg in order to be near Daisy. He threw extravagant parties to get her attention, but she never came. Now that he's connected with those who know her, he will begin the task of demystifying the fantasy as he pursues her love, once again and for the last time.

THE GREAT GATSBY

Setting: Map Project

Directions: Form small groups of 2-3 and then using the descriptions in the novel, design a map of the setting. Remember that the setting was created in Fitzgerald's mind and only he knows exactly what it looks like.

Not all groups will create maps that look alike, just like not all students will think a poem is about the same thing. You may use real maps of New York to get situated. If your copy of the novel includes the fictional map, do not look at it. This assignment is partially meant to help you pay attention to detail and the setting when you read.

Objective:
To create a map of the setting used in Fitzgerald's *The Great Gatsby* based on the descriptions given in the novel.

Below is a list of the required areas on the map. Page numbers are from the most recent pagination from Scribner:

1. East Egg (pgs. 5-6)—Nonfictional correlation is Sands Point on Long Island
2. Buchanan's house (pgs. 6 - 7)
3. West Egg (pgs. 4 - 5)—Nonfictional correlation is Kings Point on Long Island
4. Gatsby's house (pg. 5)
5. Nick's house (pg. 5)
6. Long Island Sound (pg. 5)
7. Valley of Ashes (pg. 23)—Check out the inspiration for the Valley of Ashes: http://www.litkicks.com/InGatsbysTracks#.U7NBty9YhAk
8. Railroad tracks and motor road (pg. 23)
9. Wilson's garage/house (pgs. 24 -25)
10. New York (pg. 4, 23)
11. Tom and Myrtle's apartment (pgs. 28 -29)
12. Queensboro Bridge (pgs. 68-9)

Process:
1. Choose a group of 2 or 3 peers with whom you can work productively.
2. Sketch out a rough draft of the map on notebook paper. Remember your map must be based upon descriptions from novel, and not something out of your head.
3. Get the rough draft checked and approved by your teacher before creating your final map.
4. Using various art supplies, draw your map on poster or tag board, or use a computer program to generate a map with pictures and labels. If you have a Google account, you can use Google Earth to create your map. Here are the instructions for setting this up: http://www.google.com/earth/outreach/tutorials/custommaps.html . More savvy mapping technicians can use ArcGIS: http://video.arcgis.com/watch/253/create-a-map.

THE GREAT GATSBY

Map Evaluation

Group Members:_____

Labels Required -- _____ points each:

1. ____ Buchanan's House on East Egg
2. ____ Gatsby's House on West Egg
3. ____ Nick's House on West Egg
4. ____ Long Island Sound
5. ____ Valley of Ashes (Now the site of Flushing Meadows-Corona Park)
6. ____ Railroad tracks and motor road
7. ____ Wilson's Garage/House w/ Eckleburg billboard
8. ____ Manhattan Island
9. ____ Tom and Myrtle's apartment
10. ____ Queensboro Bridge

TOTAL -- _____/_____

_____/_____ Correctly rendered and accurately presented

_____/_____ Easy to read--labeled clearly

_____/_____ Colorful and pleasing to the eye

_____/_____ Teamwork -- all members worked productively together

GRAND TOTAL _____/_____

THE GREAT GATSBY

Ch. 4: Post-Discussion QUEST   NAME_____

Put the following words in their correct places in the paragraph below:

- A. Punctilious
- B. Incredulity
- C. Somnambulatory
- D. Benedictions
- E. Denizen

In writing the novel, *The Great Gatsby*, Fitzgerald was clearly (1) ____ about his diction. This novel was to be something for which he could be truly proud, worthy of care and something of rare beauty. However, only a true (2) ____ of literature seemed to recognize the novel's true worth at the time of its publication. Many were very skeptical of the novel and looked at it with (3) ____, not believing it could or ever would become a masterpiece of American literature. In fact, the novel went out of circulation (not publication) during the final years of Fitzgerald's life. It was a shame that he never got to see his signature work earn the shows of appreciation and (4) ____ it has since come to know. The world must have been in a (5) ____ state until the novel finally garnered the positive attention it deserves. Today, it is at the top of a very long list of the greatest American novels ever written.

THE GREAT GATSBY

Possible Short and Long ESSAY Questions for Chapter Four:

SHORT ESSAYS:

1. <u>DICTION</u>: Chapter four opens with the following sentence: "On Sunday morning <u>while church bells rang in the villages alongshore</u>, the <u>world and its mistress</u> returned to Gatsby's house and <u>twinkled hilariously</u> on his lawn." Write a brief analysis of this opening. Focus especially on Fitzgerald's **use of diction** in phrases such as "church bells rang," "the world and its mistress" and "twinkled hilariously". Be sure to explain the effect of the **juxtaposition** (position of phrases near each other) between the villages alongshore and the world and its mistress.

2. <u>JUXTAPOSITION</u>: Meyer Wolfsheim tells Nick the story of Rosy Rosenthal and how he was shot outside the old Metropole, a restaurant "filled with faces dead and gone." As a follow-up to his recount of this event, Nick remembers that "Four of them [the gunmen] were electrocuted." Wolfsheim replies, "Five, with Becker" and then follows up with "I understand you're looking for a business gonnegtion." Nick's narration continues: "The **juxtaposition** of these two remarks was startling." (1) **What is being juxtaposed?** OR **To which two remarks is he referring?** and (2) **Why is the juxtaposition startling?**

3. <u>CONNOTATION</u>: Nick says, "I remembered, of course, that the World's Series had been fixed in 1919, but if I had thought of it at all I would have thought of it as a thing that merely *happened*, the end of some inevitable chain. It never occurred to me that **one man** could start to play with the faith of fifty million people—**with the single mindedness of a burglar blowing a safe**." What are the **connotations** of Nick's comparison of Wolfsheim fixing the World Series to a "burglar blowing a safe"?

LONG ESSAY:

How does the **setting of the novel** reflect the characters and their way of life, values, concerns and actions? Write about ONE of the following setting/character pairs:
- East Egg and Tom and Daisy Buchanan;
- West Egg and Gatsby (as well as his party goers)
- The Valley of Ashes and George and Myrtle Wilson.

THE GREAT GATSBY

Chapter Five

Pre-Reading Journal Question:

- If you could relive any moment in your life, what moment would you choose? Why?

Vocabulary Review: In chapter three, you will encounter the following words. For each word, find its definition and write a sentence using the word correctly. Be sure there is enough information in your sentence so your teacher can tell that you understand *how* the word is used. **Do not simply repeat the meaning of your word in the sentence.** Identify its part of speech as written below (i.e., adjective, noun, verb, adverb):

- Vitality
- Confounding
- Rendered
- Tactlessly
- Grave (as an adjective)

Preview of Class Discussion:

1. Very generally, what happened in today's chapter? Begin by listing three-to-five events and then add whatever strikes your memory. Put the events in order.

2. How do Gatsby's feelings change throughout the chapter, before, during, and after his meeting with Daisy?

3. What might be the significance or importance of the changing weather patterns? Find passages that support your assertions.

4. What might be the significance or importance of the defunct clock, which Gatsby knocks over, but then catches? Find passages that support your assertions.

5. Explain why Nick wondered whether the "colossal significance of that light had now vanished forever".

6. What do you think Daisy is feeling throughout her meeting with Gatsby, at first, during, and toward the end of the chapter? What do you think of Gatsby's efforts to reconnect with his old love? Do you think she appreciates this effort? Or is Gatsby setting himself up for heartbreak?

7. What themes do you see developing in this chapter?

THE GREAT GATSBY

Ch. 5: Post-Reading, Pre-Discussion Quiz   Name_____

DIRECTIONS: Answer the following questions on a separate sheet of paper.

1. How did Gatsby behave just prior to his meeting with Daisy?

2. How did Gatsby feel as he was showing Daisy his house?

3. What was Daisy's reaction when Gatsby threw all of his shirts into the middle of the room?

4. What did Nick mean when he wondered whether the "colossal significance of that light had now vanished forever"?

5. What was the weather like during the initial (first) phase of Gatsby's meeting with Daisy?

THE GREAT GATSBY

CHAPTER FIVE: Pre-Discussion Critical Summary for the Teacher

Terms connected to chapter five: symbol, theme, motif, extended metaphor

Events: At Gatsby's urging, Nick arranges a meeting with his cousin, Daisy, and tells her not to bring Tom. Gatsby makes arrangements to fix up Nick's little rental house and to have the lawn mowed. Upon Daisy's moment of arrival, it is raining, and Gatsby is extremely nervous and almost ready to abort the entire plan to connect with Daisy. Nick calms him down and reminds him that Daisy is nervous, too. At the end of the meeting at Nick's house, Gatsby is elated, and Daisy is emotional (she has been crying). Gatsby then gives Daisy and Nick a tour of his house, and she remarks upon his beautiful shirts with stormy emotion.

Significant passages: In this chapter, there are plentiful opportunities to discuss themes and symbols. In fact, the narration deals very specifically with a few, even going so far as to interpret them for us:

- An obvious case is the (1) **green light**, which was once a starry, untouchable dream for Gatsby. Now, after having made the connection with Daisy in person, the green light has been reduced to its more mundane proportions. Nick wonders whether the "colossal significance of that light had now vanished forever" (93).
- Another significant passage comes in the form of the (2) **defunct clock**, which Gatsby manages to knock over, only to save it from crashing to the floor (86). The connections are fairly obvious, but poignant: Gatsby is attempting to revert time to its pre-Tom era. Can this be done? The question is, what signifies a *falling* clock? Will Gatsby fumble his renewed relationship with Daisy? In fact, the clock metaphor is carried through so much of the chapter, that one could really call it an **extended metaphor**, and because it returns in subsequent chapters in the support of the ongoing theme of turning back time or reliving the past, we can safely call it a **motif**.
- Another is Daisy's obsession with (3) **Gatsby's shirts** (92). Clearly, her reaction is overblown, which leads one to consider whether she is not truly reacting to the shirts, but is simply experiencing a flustered state of emotional levity, combined with deeper feeling of sadness or remorse. Could she already understand, if dimly, the complexities and futility of a 1920s wife leaving her husband for a former lover? Or does she have the sense that she made an irreversible, bad choice in not waiting for Gatsby before marrying Tom? Gatsby is certainly not considering either of these possibilities.
- Finally, (4) **the weather** seems to reflect Gatsby's own emotional upheavals in this chapter. When he's nervous and Daisy cries, it rains; when he and Daisy truly make an emotional connection and he is "glowing", the sun comes out; and when Gatsby stands with Daisy to look at a pink sky (with Daisy imagining pushing him around *playfully* in the cradle of a cloud), he is in a state Nick

describes as "running down like an overwound clock". Nick tells us Gatsby, indeed, passes through three stages (88-9).

THE GREAT GATSBY

Symbol Activity: Chapters Four and Five

DIRECTIONS: In a small group of about three, write a **children's book** about a day in the life of a symbol from chapter five of *The Great Gatsby*. Here are the rules for successful completion of this little project:

1. The day should cover the ***symbol's "participation" in Gatsby's reunion*** with Daisy and its use as a backdrop to reflect what is going on in the scene.
2. It should be written from the **symbol's perspective or viewpoint**, and ***should not*** give a comprehensive account of every detail.
3. The "Intangible ***Subject***" (or abstract idea or theme) in the comparison should be made ***very clear***, clear enough to make a child of six understand its basic meaning (relatively speaking).
4. You may complete this small project by hand or with the computer. However, please ***make it simple***.
5. Include ***large*** illustrations (Pictures do not have to be artistic masterpieces. This is just an experimental exercise.).
6. The performance/class reading **time limits are between two and three minutes** (including set up and take down—if any). No less, no more.
7. You **may not go over 10 pages** and must limit your word count on each to page to no more than **20**.

When you are finished, you will read your book to the class. You should consider adding background music or even a performance component to the telling of the story. Again: do not make this too elaborate. It should be short, sweet, and to the point. Performance components might include shadow or finger puppets. Be sure to include some form of the object, itself, in your presentation.

(1) Make a list of the three symbols (total) from chapters four and five. These symbols should be well developed. List your three symbols (objects) under "Tangible Item" on the left, while the subject of the comparison should go on the right under "Intangible Subject":

Tangible Items   **Intangible Subjects/Ideas**

E.g. *A Rose*   E.g. *Love*

(2) Next, try brainstorming ideas for these symbols. Then, choose the symbol that will be the topic of your children's book.

(3) Before doing too much with it, be sure you have a deep enough understanding of how the symbol you chose helps to make an important point about the theme. Reread the passage concerning the symbol you chose. Discuss with your partners how you will describe this scene from the symbol's point of view.

THE GREAT GATSBY

Ch. 5: Post-Discussion Quest   Name_____

Match each of the following words to its correct part of speech in the right-hand column.

        1. ____Vitality   A. Adjective

        2. ____Confounding   B. Noun

        3. ____Rendered   C. Adverb

        4. ____Tactlessly   D. Verb

        5. ____ Vital

        6. ____ Confound

        7. ____ Tactless

        8. ____ Tact

        9. ____ Grave (As in: "Her mood was '*grave*'.")

       10. ____ Gravely

Now, put the words above into their correct places in the following sentences. Be sure to spell each word just as it should be spelled in the sentence (i.e. Use the correct part of speech.):

11. _____ "The girl ___ told the woman sitting across from her that she must have gained a lot of weight since she last saw her."

12. _____ "The dog was ___ helpless when its owners left him in the backyard for the duration of their two-week vacation. When they returned, they found that the dog had been taken to a shelter."

13. _____ "After a blood transfusion, the man's ___ returned to him, and he felt like a new person."

14. _____ "I found the movie to be very ___, but very intriguing at the same time. We are still trying to figure out what really happened to the female character in the end."

15. _____ "The man walked ___ into the doctor's office, for he expected to get a bad diagnosis."

THE GREAT GATSBY

Directions: **Open Book Essay:** Submit a well-written essay of between four and six paragraphs on **a** symbol and how it functions, very specifically, to support a theme in chapter four or five of *The Great Gatsby*. Include a thesis statement and a conclusion.

Respond to the following questions. Then, using your responses and a collection of quotes from the chapter, formulate a ***cogent*** and ***coherent*** explication of how the symbol is used in the chapter.

Here are some questions to get you thinking:

1) Does the symbol you chose define or merely reinforce the meaning of the story? Explain.
2) Do you feel that Fitzgerald wrote the chapter and then went back and stuck in symbols? Or are they well integrated into the story? How?
3) Identify quotes that will show how the symbol helps the reader understand the meaning and theme. Follow up with an explanation.

THE GREAT GATSBY

Chapter Six: *The Great Gatsby*

Pre-Reading Journal Question:

- If you were to *re*live the most magical time in your life, would it have the same effect upon you as it did before? Can you repeat the past? Explain.

Vocabulary Review: In chapter six, you will encounter most of the following words. For each word, find its definition and write a sentence using the word correctly. Be sure there is enough information in your sentence so your teacher can tell that you understand *how* the word is used. **Do not simply repeat the meaning of your word in the sentence.** Identify its part of speech as written below (i.e., adjective, noun, verb, adverb):

- Meretricious
- Ineffable
- Gaudiness
- Euphemism
- Menagerie
- Dilatory
- Obtrusive
- Synesthesia (as it is used in literature)
- Motif (as it is used in literature)

Preview of Class Discussion:

1. Why does James Gatz change his name to Jay Gatsby at age seventeen?

2. Why is Gatsby so interested in seeing more of Tom?

3. Why do Tom and Daisy's attendance at the party change Nick's experience of it?

4. How does Daisy's experience of Gatsby's party affect Gatsby's feelings? Why does he say, "I feel far away from her. It's hard to make her understand" ?

5. Nick tells Gatsby that one "cannot repeat the past." What is Gatsby's reaction to this? Do you agree with Nick? Explain?

6. Do you think it is okay that Gatsby is pursuing Daisy? Explain.

7. What are your predictions for the relationship between Gatsby and Daisy? Offer textual support for your predictions.

THE GREAT GATSBY

Ch. 6: Post-Reading, <u>Pre-Discussion</u> Quiz   Name_____

DIRECTIONS: Answer the following questions on a separate sheet of paper:

1. How did the REAL story of Gatsby differ from the one he told Nick?

2. Who is Dan Cody, and what was his influence upon Gatsby?

3. What did Daisy think of Gatsby's party?

4. What was Gatsby's criterion for measuring the degree of success of his party?

5. When Nick told Gatsby that one "can't repeat the past", how does Gatsby respond?

THE GREAT GATSBY

CHAPTER SIX: Pre-Discussion Critical Summary for the Teacher

Terms: Synesthesia; recurring motif

Commentary: In chapter six, Nick describes Gatsby's past in terms of two different people: James Gatz and Jay Gatsby. Although these are the same person, there is a striking difference between them. The narration reads: "It was **James Gatz** who had been loafing along the beach that afternoon in a torn green jersey and a pair of canvas pants, but it was already **Jay Gatsby** who borrowed a rowboat, pulled out to the *Tuolomee*, and informed Cody that a wind might catch him and break him up in half an hour" (98). The point, here, is to highlight Gatz's intentions to reject his own humble beginnings and to embrace a greatness far beyond even the most ambitious of dreams, dreams that do not begin and end simply with wealth and power. Neither does Gatz want to be famous; his ambition is on a divine order, as "a son of God" who "must be about His Father's business" (98). Although the novice reader might take the reference a tad too literally, or jump immediately to a simple comparison to Jesus, one might want to give attention to the rest of the sentence, which extends the notion of "His father's business" as "the service of a vast, vulgar, and meretricious beauty" (98). If students know their vocabulary, they will agree with Nick that this sort of *meretricious* ambition is "just the sort of Jay Gatsby that a seventeen-year-old boy would be likely to invent" (98). However, the reader is likely to agree that Gatsby is faithful to this conception of success "to the end." One can forgive the seventeen-year-old for trying to bring about *meretricious* dreams; but can one forgive such pursuits in adulthood? Does Gatsby's faithfulness to these dreams render him more culpable than he is laudable? Though his ambition is highly romantic and beyond ferocious (god-like), it has its limits. In what sense is it limited? In what sense is it vast?

Again, we have the clock ***motif*** in a very dense and stunning passage (99). This is the second time in a short period we have encountered the well-deployed symbol of the clock (in addition to the green light and other concrete elements). Two particularly loaded sentences read: "A universe of ineffable gaudiness spun itself out in his brain **while the clock ticked on the washstand** and the moon soaked with wet light his tangled clothes upon the floor. . . . For a while these reveries provided an outlet for his imagination; they were a satisfactory hint of the unreality of reality, a promise that the rock of the world was founded securely on a fairy's wing" (99). (Notice the deft use of ***synesthesia*** in the underlined portion above)

One might point out the juxtaposition of the boy dreaming in his bed of better circumstances while the clock is ticking (or time is passing) on the washstand. He has only so much time to make these dreams a reality and not a moment more. One can't help but recall the image of Gatsby finally winding down like an overwrought clock upon reconnecting with Daisy in the previous chapter (92). He is truly an epic figure, much like Icarus, who flies dangerously close to the sun. All that remains now is the tragic or epic fall, or the winding down of a tightly wound clock. On an initial read, an undercurrent of

62

foreboding ought now to pursue the reader through chapters six, seven, and eight. For, indeed, it is little more than a decade after the Gatz boy becomes awake to his dream that a reinvented Gatsby meets a very quick demise. Gatsby's youthful reveries are thus "a satisfactory hint of the unreality of reality, a promise that the rock of the world was founded securely on a fairy's wing." Gatsby may have jettisoned the reminders of his humble origins, but he was never able to remove his veil of illusion, even as he gained wealth, notoriety, and misrecognized the fleeting affections of Mrs. Tom Buchanan. But we are not there, just yet.

In the remainder of the chapter, Tom comes twice to Gatsby's, first in an unexpected visit with Sloan and a "pretty woman" on horseback (101-3). While there, Gatsby announces almost aggressively that he has met Daisy. Disturbed, Tom later returns with Daisy and Jordan for one of Gatsby's parties, declaring he will discover the truth behind Gatsby. In fact, he suspects correctly that Gatsby is a bootlegger. When Tom and Daisy do show up, Daisy does not enjoy herself. Daisy is turned off by the shows of raw emotion on the part of the guests, for she is used to expressing herself in subtle "gestures," while Gatsby's guests, many who come from immigrant backgrounds, express themselves in ways that seem too extravagant, tactless, and almost obscene to Daisy: "She was appalled by West Egg, this unprecedented 'place' that Broadway had begotten upon a Long Island fishing village—appalled by its raw vigor that chafed under the old *euphemisms* and by the too *obtrusive* fate that herded its inhabitants along a short-cut from nothing to nothing" (107). Gatsby is depressed that Daisy was so turned off, and says that he will "fix everything just the way it was before" (110). He expects to repeat the past and to restore it to the way things were before Daisy married Tom. Nick warns Gatsby not to expect too much of Daisy, in essence, to discard four years of marriage and her role as a mother: "I wouldn't ask too much of her . . . . You can't repeat the past." And with the hubristic confidence of a Trojan warrior, Gatsby resounds, "Why of course you can!" (110).

THE GREAT GATSBY

Recurring Motif, Chapter Six   **CLASS ACTIVITY: A Musical Approach**

For the teacher:

To review, a literary *motif* is a recurring element in a work of literature. Although one can easily call it a theme, it is, most of the time, a concrete symbol that promotes or forwards a theme in a literary work, and does so repeatedly. When you see an image, an object, an agency, or an action repeated, it's time to stop and ask: Why? In *The Great Gatsby*, some of what we've already identified as stand-alone symbols in early chapters are now being repeated in subsequent chapters. At this point, we can begin to broaden our interpretation of some of these symbols as recurring *motifs*.

A literary motif is not unlike a musical *leitmotif*. If you have never studied music theory, leitmotifs are, simply, short musical melodies that coincide with a character in a story (like in opera). Each time the character (or entity) takes the stage or shows up in the piece, that character's melody is woven into the musical composition. The concept began with the 19th-century German composer **Richard Wagner**, but there are plenty of accessible examples in contemporary film scores that students will likely already recognize. For instance, **John Williams**, the *Star Wars* trilogy composer, employs "The Imperial March" to signal anything related to Darth Vader. Similarly, **Robert Shore**, *The Lord of the Rings* trilogy composer, employs the Gondor motif; the motif plays along with Gondor's dialogue.

Another very accessible piece you might use to teach the concept is **Sergei Prokoviev's** *Peter and the Wolf*. It is fun to listen to and very easy to locate its leitmotifs: The sound of the flute, for instance, represents the bird; the oboe the duck; the clarinet the cat; the bassoon the Grandfather; the French horns the wolf; the string quartet Peter, etc.

A wonderful way to spark interest in examining the literary motif is to **compare and contrast** how motifs are used in **musical scores** and in **literary works**. I would talk about this in a whole-class discussion after listening, together, to parts of one or more of the pieces mentioned above. Then, I would ask the students to work exclusively with *The Great Gatsby* using the following steps:

1. Make a list of symbols and other elements that have recurred in the novel so far. Students should come up with the green light, the weather, the clock, Daisy's voice, and driving (which will lead to the car crash motif in the chapter eight).
2. Choose to work with ONE of the recurring motifs.
3. Using a graphic organizer (such as a spider web), brainstorm the reasons for the motif in *The Great Gatsby*.
4. Compare notes with other members of the class or in a whole-group discussion.

THE GREAT GATSBY

Ch. 6: Post-Discussion QUEST   Name_____

   A. Chafed
   B. Meretricious
   C. Ineffable
   D. Gaudiness
   E. Euphemism
   F. Menagerie
   G. Dilatory
   H. Obtrusive

DIRECTIONS: Put the words above into their correct places in the following sentences. Some words may work acceptably in some sentences, but others will work BETTER. Be sure to choose the absolute BEST word for each sentence:

1. The military term "collateral damage" is a ____ for the unintentional killing of civilians, which can easily include children and the elderly.

2. We saw a ____ of animals at the circus.

3. I was deeply impressed by your ____ performance of Judy Garland's "Somewhere Over the Rainbow". Words cannot describe what a beautiful voice you have.

4. I was distracted and annoyed by your ____ interruptions during today's class.

5. The ____ boy tiptoed quietly into every class about ten minutes late.

6. The ____ delights of Las Vegas impress some people. But others prefer the organic delights of the mountains, the ocean, and the sights and sounds of natural wonders.

7. The ____ of Las Vegas, with its flamboyant shows, flashy lights, and tawdry amusements, is a bit much for some people, but not all people.

8. I should have never worn my new shoes on a five-mile hike, for they have ____ against my skin, and now I have several blisters.

MULTIPLE CHOICE:

____ 9. Which of the following is **NOT** a recurring motif in *The Great Gatsby*?

   A. The Clock
   B. The Green Light
   C. Cars/driving
   D. Cemeteries

THE GREAT GATSBY

_____ 10. Which of the following literary techniques is **NOT** being used in this sentence from chapter six: "A universe of ineffable gaudiness spun itself out in his brain while the clock ticked on the washstand and the moon soaked with wet light."

A. Recurring Motif
B. Alliteration
C. Synesthesia
D. Imagery

On a separate sheet of paper: Explain the following passage from chapter six. First, put the scene into its context (Explain the subject of the passage and what is going on at this point in the story.). More importantly, be sure to explain Fitzgerald's word choices (diction) as indicated by the **bolded** words. What meaning do they carry?

But the rest offended her—and inarguably, because it wasn't a **gesture** but an emotion. She was appalled by West Egg, this unprecedented "place" that Broadway had begotten upon a Long Island fishing village—appalled by its **raw vigor** that **chafed** under the **old euphemisms** and by the too obtrusive fate that **herded** its inhabitants along a short-cut from nothing to nothing. She saw something awful in the very simplicity she failed to understand.

THE GREAT GATSBY

Chapter Seven

Pre-Reading Journal Questions: Choose one:

1. Have you ever gotten sick and tired of hanging around a specific group of people? Why did you get sick of them? What did you do? Explain.
2. How far would you go to protect the person you love most in the world? Would you lie for this person? Would you cover up a crime he or she committed? How far would you go before you *would* no longer protect this person?

Vocabulary Review: In chapter seven, you will encounter most of the following words. For each word, find its definition and write a sentence using the word correctly. Be sure there is enough information in your sentence so your teacher can tell that you understand *how* the word is used. **Do not simply repeat the meaning of your word in the sentence.** Identify its part of speech as written below (i.e., adjective, noun, verb, adverb):

- Relinquish
- Intermittent
- Sensuous
- Magnanimous
- Portentous
- Menacing
- Precipitately
- Situational Irony (Literary Term)
- Foreshadowing (Literary Term)

Preview of Class Discussion:

1. How have things changed at Gatsby's house? Why?

2. Why does Gatsby want to invite Nick over to the Buchanans for a get together with the entire group, including Jordan?

3. What is Daisy's likely purpose in making a display of her affection for Gatsby?

4. How does Gatsby react when Daisy's daughter appears? What does this say about his plans for Daisy?

5. Why does Tom insist on driving Gatsby's car, despite Gatsby's distaste for the idea? Why does Tom call Gatsby's car a "circus wagon"?

THE GREAT GATSBY

6. What happens when Tom stops for gas at Wilson's Garage? Why is George sick? Whom does Nick see up in the window over the garage? What do you think has happened in the Wilson household in the past few hours?

7. How does Wilson's announcement that he and his wife are moving west affect Tom?

8. Why is Gatsby so upset when Daisy tells him that she did love Tom "once—but I loved you too"?

9. How does Daisy react to Tom's attempts to embarrass Gatsby about his alleged Oxford pedigree and business dealings? How does Gatsby react to Daisy's reaction? What do you think of Daisy's reaction?

10. What do you think was the purpose of including the sound of wedding music and festivities during Tom and Gatsby's confrontation at the Plaza Hotel?

11. What, do you think, is the significance of the fact that the weather is so hot in chapter seven? "The next day was broiling, almost the last, certainly the warmest, of the summer."

12. What do you think is the significance of Nick suddenly realizing that it was his 30th birthday? Pay attention to the words that follow.

13. How does each one of the characters (George, Gatsby, Tom, Jordan, Daisy) react to Myrtle's fatal accident? How might you interpret these reactions? OR, What does it say about each of them?

14. Nick says, "I'd had enough of all of them for one day." Why is Nick so sick and tired of the entire group? Would you be at this point?

15. Why do you think Nick does not tell Gatsby that he saw Daisy and Tom "conspiring together"?

THE GREAT GATSBY

Ch. 7: Post-Reading, <u>Pre-Discussion</u> Quiz   Name_____

1. ____ Why did Gatsby fire all of his servants?
   A. Because the kitchen looked like a pigsty.
   B. Because he wanted to remove anyone who might tell of his affair with Daisy.
   C. Because he wanted to do something for the family of brothers and sisters who took their place.
   D. Because Daisy didn't like Gatsby's current servants.

2. ____ Who drives Gatsby's car on the way *in* to New York City?
   A. Gatsby
   B. Daisy
   C. Nick
   D. Tom
   E. Jordan

3. ____ What was the weather like on the day of the trip into New York City and to the Plaza Hotel?
   A. Stormy
   B. Mild
   C. Hot
   D. Unusually cold

4. ____ Who was driving Gatsby's car on the way *back* to Long Island?
   A. Daisy
   B. Nick
   C. Tom
   D. Gatsby

5. ____ Given Gatsby's retelling of the accident to Nick, what is the most likely reason Myrtle ran out into the road (right before she is hit by the car)?
   A. Because her husband kicked her out of the house for having an affair.
   B. Because she wanted to catch the train before it pulled away.
   C. Because she saw the familiar yellow car and wanted to intercept it.
   D. Because she was aiming to commit suicide.

6. ____ Why, specifically, does Gatsby wait outside of Daisy's house on the night of the accident?
   A. Because he wanted to make sure Tom did not harm Daisy.
   B. Because Daisy is supposed to sneak out to speak with him after they all go to bed.
   C. Because he wants to make sure Wilson does not come looking for Daisy.
   D. Because he and Daisy are supposed to run away together.

THE GREAT GATSBY

CHAPTER SEVEN: Pre-Discussion Critical Summary for the Teacher

Terms: Situational Irony, Climax

"The lights in his house fail to go on one Saturday night" (113): Now that Gatsby has been reunited with Daisy, he no longer needs to throw extravagant parties to get her attention; she's already at his house, and frequently. Furthermore, Gatsby has fired all of his former servants to avoid gossip and has put in their place a family connected to Wolfsheim. They are neither friendly nor good housekeepers, but Wolfsheim owes them for "something". But, alas, Gatsby believes he has Daisy. All that remains is to get rid of Tom. Chapter seven is highly climactic. It is often referred to as "Showdown at the Plaza Hotel" and for good reasons. It is where Tom and Gatsby effectively duel for Daisy. Fittingly, it is the hottest day of the summer, and one of the last (114), for emotions will heat to dangerous degrees before Gatsby takes his death plunge (recall the Icarus story) in the next chapter. Again, we have another reference to the **weather motif**.

"Where's daddy?" (117): Gatsby calls to invite Nick over to Daisy's house. The entire group will be there and we suspect, with Nick, that this will be the occasion to break the news to Tom. However, Daisy seems mostly to want to taunt Tom with her affections for Gatsby, making a display of kissing him in front of the group (116). In the midst of such displays, Daisy's daughter appears and Gatsby looks astonished. Nick tells us, "I don't think he had ever really believed in its existence before" (117), for Gatsby's dreams do not include the inconvenient truths connected to Mrs. Buchanan. He does not even believe, effectively, that a *Mrs.* Buchanan exists; only a Daisy, who happens to be married to the wrong man, exists. Tom is understandably and predictably alarmed, however, and realizes that Daisy and Gatsby have been secretly seeing each other: "She had told him [Gatsby] that she loved him, and Tom Buchanan saw" (119). This leads to his willingness to play the game, to go to town, to let the showdown begin: "All right. . . . I'm perfectly willing to go to town. Come on—we're all going to town. . . . What's the matter, anyhow? If we're going to town, let's start" (119). In this scene, Tom's eyes are "flashing between Gatsby and his wife" (119).

"Let's have some gas!" (123): Tom has not paid much notice to Daisy's own illicit activities before, likely because he was juggling his own ongoing affair with Myrtle. However, while stopping to gas up Gatsby's yellow "circus wagon," he realizes suddenly that he is on the verge of losing both his wife and his mistress, for a physically ill (and jealously "green") George Wilson informs him that he wants or needs to sell Tom's car because he is moving Myrtle out west whether she wants to go, or not. As it turns out, George knows, now, about Myrtle's affair, but he does not know with whom she is having it. In the meantime, Myrtle is trapped upstairs and, behind a windowpane, seething with jealousy at the sight of Jordan, whom she takes to be Daisy (124). It is important to help the students notice this section, because it adds credibility to the notion that Myrtle later attempts to stop the car, since she thinks Tom is still driving it.

THE GREAT GATSBY

"Whatever intentions, whatever courage she had had, were definitely gone" (135): Finally, while at the Plaza Hotel, the showdown begins with the pronouncement from Gatsby that "Your wife doesn't love you. . . . She's never loved you. She loves me" (130). Tom scoffs at this confession and uses his new knowledge of Gatsby's bootlegging practices to cut him down in front of Daisy, who is "drawing further and further into herself" (134). Gatsby tries to defend himself, but is ineffectual, "and only the dead dream fought on as the afternoon slipped away, trying to touch what was no longer tangible, struggling unhappily, undespairingly, toward that lost voice across the room" (134). Daisy's voice, which was earlier described as a "deathless song" has now lost its animation, and the dream flickers out too suddenly in light of Gatsby's heroic desires. And for what? All too quickly, Daisy's resolve is easily extinguished. However, Tom sends Gatsby and Daisy packing in the familiar yellow circus wagon "toward death through the cooling twilight" (136) to stew in Gatsby's defeat.

"Wilson'll have a little business at last" (137): We do not see Myrtle's accident, but we experience its aftermath through the eyes of Nick. As with all of the passages in the novel, the scene expands in all of its literary bloom, pregnant with interpretive possibilities: (A) Myrtle's fatal injuries are morbidly sensuous, with her naked breast detached and dangling to one side, and the red blood dripping from the corners of her open mouth, draining her vitality and once teeming sexuality (137); (B) it is not Gatsby who runs into Myrtle, but Daisy, Myrtle's nemesis, or the other woman in Myrtle's eyes; (C) and while Gatsby's car does the physical damage, it is Tom, at bottom, whose careless actions make the death scene possible and, in turn, the subsequent deaths of Wilson and Gatsby.

"I'd had enough of all of them" (142): It is revealing, however, to examine each of the character's reactions to Myrtle's death. It tells much about who they are and what they care about, to a degree. There is always the possibility that fleeting sentimentalism, for instance, may be at the heart of Tom's grief over the shocking and violent death of his mistress. In the end, Nick has had enough of the whole gang and their drama. He is even soured on Jordan, perhaps by association, but also because she seems exceedingly more disturbed by Nick's leaving for home while the night is still young than she is by the terrible carnage of a fatal accident. Nick, on the other hand, is struck, even before the accident, by the realization that he is now thirty, and that time is ticking "with the promise of a decade of loneliness"(135). Perhaps that plays significantly into his distaste even for his friend, Gatsby, whose only consideration is, once again, with Daisy's welfare (143) and keeping watch over her house out of an empty attempt to keep her safe from Tom, even as she now sits at the kitchen table with that same Tom, "conspiring" (145).

Situational Irony: The ironies in the chapter are many.
- First, it is highly ironic that Tom should be shaming Gatsby for his undercover operations and Oxford story when Tom consistently cheats on his wife with

another man's wife, Jordan cheats in major golfing tournaments, and Daisy's daily comportment is a barely veiled attempt to hide her disappointments.
- Secondly, it is ironic that Mendelssohn's Wedding March be playing as a sort of backdrop to Tom and Gatsby's duel over Daisy at the Plaza Hotel; as one couple is breaking up, another couple is getting married; the entire fight is enacted to the music, almost like a Hollywood movie. Is it perhaps Tom and Daisy's marriage renewal?
- Thirdly, Tom, Wilson, and Gatsby are on the verge of losing their romantic or domestic partners at the same time.
- Fourth: Myrtle makes at least two ironic misrecognitions. She mistakes Jordan for Daisy, and she mistakes Gatsby's car for Tom's car. She dies because of a simple case of misidentification.
- The resolution to the novel is fast approaching, where things will work out, ironically, to Tom's favor, as if he, himself, had written the novel's final chapters to reflect his own best scenario. Already, in chapter seven, Tom sends Gatsby and Daisy home "toward death" to inadvertently "off" his mistress. Ironically, this accident makes it possible to neatly sweep away the past in one fell swoop and reunite with Daisy.

THE GREAT GATSBY

Situational Irony

Situational Irony occurs when the outcome of a situation is not what is expected. In fact, it is usually the opposite of what's expected. Situational Irony can be done for a humorous or serious effect. Here are a few good examples of situational irony in literature from **YourDictionary.com**:

Situational Irony in Literature

- *Romeo and Juliet* by William Shakespeare - Romeo finds Juliet drugged and assumes she is dead. He kills himself then she awakens, sees that he is dead and kills herself.
- *The Gift of the Magi* by O. Henry - The wife cuts her long hair and sells it to buy her husband a pocket watch chain. He sells the watch to buy her a hair accessory.
- In the Greek play, *Oedipus Rex* by Sophocles, Oedipus kills his father and marries his mother, unaware of his true familial relationship to both. The mistake occurs because, as a baby, he (Oedipus) was left to die by his father because of a prophecy foretelling this very event. Instead, baby Oedipus is rescued and adopted, only to grow up, kill his blood father and marry his blood mother.
- *The Rime of the Ancient Mariner* by Coleridge - Water, water, every where, And all the boards did shrink ; Water, water, every where, Nor any drop to drink.

In a small group of three or four, discuss situational irony in chapter seven. Together, come up with a list of three cases of situational irony from chapter seven to share with the whole class. Then, evaluate together each group's list of examples.

THE GREAT GATSBY

Ch. 7: Post-Discussion QUEST Name_____

Match the following vocabulary words to their synonyms:

1. ___Relinquish   A. Stimulating; luxurious
2. ___Intermittent   B. Rashly; hastily
3. ___Sensuous   C. Surrender; renounce
4. ___Magnanimous   D. Momentous; significant
5. ___Portentous   E. Threatening; intimidating
6. ___Menacing   F. Generous; noble
7. ___Precipitately   G. Sporadic; irregular

8. ____ Which part of the plot is chapter 7?
    A. Exposition (when important info is introduced. The conflict is introduced.)
    B. Rising action (when the tension builds because of the conflict)
    C. Climax (when the conflict is confronted, which ushers in a new direction)
    D. Falling Action (when the consequences of the climactic events ensue)

9. ____ On the return trip from the Plaza Hotel, Nick says of himself, Tom, and Jordan, "We drove on toward death through the cooling twilight." In this short sentence, Nick is making use of all of the following literary devices, **EXCEPT**
    A. Character foiling
    B. Foreshadowing
    C. Multisensory Imagery
    D. Recurring Motif

10. ____ All of the following are examples of situational irony, **EXCEPT**
    A. While Tom and Gatsby fight over Daisy at the Plaza Hotel, one can hear the jubilant voices and music from a wedding in progress downstairs.
    B. The same Tom who shames Gatsby for his undercover operations and Oxford story is the same Tom who consistently cheats on his wife with another man's wife.
    C. Though she hopes for more, Nick rebuffs Jordan at the end of chapter seven.
    D. Daisy just happens to be the one who mows over the other woman, Tom's mistress.

THE GREAT GATSBY

Chapter Eight

Pre-Reading Journal Questions: Choose One:

1. Can a person become insane? Or must he/she be born predisposed to insanity? If so, why? If not, why not? Explain.

2. The following question is from http://www.philosophytalk.org:
"What difference does it make if the person who commits a crime is, in one way or another, mentally ill? Does this make punishment illegitimate?" Should a person who is insane go to prison or be sent to therapy?

Vocabulary Review: In chapter seven, you will encounter most of the following words. For each word, find its definition and write a sentence using the word correctly. Be sure there is enough information in your sentence so your teacher can tell that you understand *how* the word is used. **Do not simply repeat the meaning of your word in the sentence**. Identify its part of speech as written below (i.e., adjective, noun, verb, adverb):

In addition to the above: Make sure you are able to decline each of the first five words (e.g. from an adverb to an adjective, etc.). You will need this skill for the next QUEST:

- Ravenously
- Unscrupulously
- Stratum
- Redolent
- Amorphous
- Holocaust (the original meaning of the word)
- Character Foil (Literary Term)
- Personification (Literary Term)
- Antecedent (In grammar; sentence structure)
- Authorial Intent

Preview of Class Discussion:

1. Why does Gatsby continue to wait for Daisy?

2. Why do you think Nick chooses to share the Dan Cody story with us in chapter six when he only heard about after Myrtle's accident?

3. Why does Gatsby find that he has "committed himself to the following of a grail"?

THE GREAT GATSBY

4. Why is Nick annoyed with Jordan when she calls him at the office?

5. How would you interpret Wilson's reaction to Myrtle's death? How would you describe his state of mind?

6. What do you think is the **authorial intent** when Nick uses the word "holocaust" in the final sentence of chapter eight? "The holocaust was complete." What are the origins of the word "holocaust" and whose holocaust is it?

7. Are any of the characters alike in any way?

8. Who is most at fault for Myrtle's accident? Gatsby? Tom? Daisy? Wilson? Myrtle? Explain.

THE GREAT GATSBY

Ch. 8: Post-Reading, <u>Pre-Discussion</u> Quiz Name_____

I. TRUE or FALSE: Write out the entire word.

1. _____ Daisy couldn't wait for Gatsby because she was impatient to see her life take shape.

2. _____ Almost immediately after their honeymoon is over, Tom has an affair.

3. _____ While at work, Nick calls Jordan to try to get back together with her.

4. _____ George Wilson is a regular church-goer.

5. _____ Wilson mistakes the Doctor T.J. Eckleburg billboard for God.

6. _____ Wilson shoots Gatsby when Gatsby is where?
    A. In the shower.
    B. In the pool.
    C. On the lawn.
    D. In the library.

II. Identify the speaker of each of the following quotations from chapter eight. Use the name bank to select your answers. Some names will not be used at all.

   A. Tom   D. Nick   G. Michaelis
   B. Daisy   E. Gatsby   H. Wolfsheim
   C. Jordan   F. Wilson

7._____ They're a rotten crowd. . . . You're worth the whole damn bunch put together.

8._____ You weren't so nice to me last night.

9._____ Have you got a church you go to sometimes, George?

10._____ I'm one of these trusting fellas and I don't think any harm to *no*body, but when I get to know a thing I know it.

THE GREAT GATSBY

CHAPTER EIGHT: Pre-Discussion Critical Summary for the Teacher

Literary Concepts: Personification, Character Foil, Authorial Intent

Having made it home, Nick finds that he cannot sleep for anxiety about Gatsby's welfare (the fog horn, too, is an alert to imminent danger). He says he felt there was something he needed to warn him about (147). Nick has bad feelings about what is likely to happen to Gatsby, and so does the reader through this deft use of **foreshadowing**. Since Gatsby is not, himself, acting with a healthy dose of self-preservation, but is anxious only to hear from Daisy, Nick is perhaps feeling the insecurity for the both of them.

Gatsby, however, eagerly awaits Daisy's decision about whether she will stay with Tom or leave him. But Daisy will never call again. The readers who are less hungry for a happy ending sense this, but Gatsby clings fruitlessly to his hope that Daisy's desires reflect equally upon his own dreams. So Nick indulges Gatsby's need to talk about Daisy, and this is when he hears about Dan Cody and Gatsby's own version of his 1917 romance with Daisy (148-51). During Gatsby's deployment, the two lovers exchange letters, but Daisy soon gets impatient to see her life take shape. She can no longer wait for Gatsby and joins her life to Tom's. **Ironically**, if she had waited a little longer, she would have been reunited with Gatsby within the next two months, for while Daisy and Tom are on their honeymoon, Gatsby returns to Louisville to seek her out. He wanders about the familiar haunts he and Daisy made meaningful, aching to be touched, once again, by the warmth of her breath. There is a stunning description of a **personified** sun on Gatsby's way out of town. He is now penniless from spending his money probing the glittering residue of his lost romance. But the sun's benediction, or blessing, beautifully reflects Gatsby's associations with a divinely inspired Louisville, and one that he must leave behind:

> The track curved and now it was going away from the sun, which, as it sank lower, seemed to spread itself in benediction over the vanishing city where she had drawn her breath. He stretched out his hand desperately as if to snatch only a wisp of air, to save a fragment of the spot that she had made lovely for him. But it was all going by too fast now for his blurred eyes and he knew that he had lost that part of it, the freshest and the best, forever. (153)

Eventually, Nick hesitantly leaves for work, but not without complimenting Gatsby: "They're a rotten crowd," he yells, "You're worth the whole damn bunch put together." Nick says he's always been glad he said that, because he "disapproved of him from beginning to end" (154). It is the last time Nick would ever see Gatsby alive, standing on the very steps where he once waved to his departing guests "who guessed at his corruption" while he was "concealing his incorruptible dream" (154). Nick's contradictory attitude towards Gatsby becomes clearer now; while he disapproves of Gatsby's corrupt activities, he is admiring of the largeness of his spirit and the purity of

THE GREAT GATSBY

his dream, his unbounded and innocent love for Daisy. Nick further solidifies his disgust with the Buchanan circle in calling them a "rotten crowd." By contrast, especially, Gatsby is shown to be noble in his pursuit of money, even of living, because it is entirely for the sake of an unspoiled love, the highest emotion of any. Although Gatsby's brand of love may seem a little childlike to the wry postmodern reader, it is preferable to Tom's, which takes Daisy's affections entirely for granted, playing at life with no real sense of seriousness or urgency.

Back in New York, Nick is trying to concentrate on finances when he gets a customary phone call from Jordan. She is, of all things, upset with Nick's comportment toward her on the night of Myrtle's accident. Nick is put off by her self-absorption and apparent blindness to the value (or even the existence) of lives "below" her social and financial strata. However authentic she is in refusing to pretend she cares when she clearly does not, a politic pretense of concern would not make it worse. But in Jordan's case, it is not clear she even recognizes her own moral failing. Perhaps she does not deserve the kind of condemnation Tom deserves. It doesn't matter. Nick is beginning to lump the two, along with Daisy, together, so that their names are practically interchangeable when it comes to their collective indifference. In the previous chapter, Nick declares: "I'd had enough of all of them for one day, and suddenly that included Jordan too" (142).

In any case, the conversation between the two continues until it simply stops. Nick doesn't care: "I couldn't have talked to her across a tea-table that day if I never talked to her again in this world" (155). He is completely absorbed by his concern for Gatsby and catches the next train back to West Egg. Too late! Just as Nick is racing up Gatsby's steps, Gatsby is in his pool, bearing the force of a gunshot; and just a few steps away stands the shell of a defeated man with a gun to his head.

Wilson's own demise is central to chapter eight and to deepening and extending the reader's understanding of the kind of carnage left behind by Tom's actions. Students might benefit from drawing a **timeline of direct causes**, from the accident, itself, to the car to the showdown to Gatsby's affair with Daisy, and finally back to Tom's extra-marital pursuits, which caused Myrtle to run into the street and left Daisy primed to seek love elsewhere. Students should be counseled gently out of any circular reasoning they might invoke. For example, I've heard students say, "If Gatsby had never moved to Long Island, this would have never happened." No. The entire story would have never happened.

Wilson is a broken man in every sense: financially, romantically, psychologically, and emotionally. Furthermore, he has been cuckolded and emasculated. While murder in the first degree is unequivocally wrong, Wilson's desperation is completely within the realm of empathy. It is important that students be invited to reflect upon Wilson's own state of mind that Fitzgerald works out so carefully and painfully in chapter eight. Though having never been to church, at least while living with Myrtle, Wilson is desperate to see the just rewarded and the guilty punished. He knows by now that Tom is the culprit, and uses the eyes of Doctor T. J. Eckleburg as a token of reassurance, because they loomed constantly over the sight of two colliding worlds: "I told her she might fool me but she couldn't fool God. I took her to the window" .... Michaelis saw with a shock that he was looking at the eyes of Doctor T. J. Eckleburg" (159). But George must've lost some faith in the strength of God's eyeglasses, because he takes matters into his own hands. Or, he pretends God is leading him straight to Myrtle's abuser and killer. However, the first-time reader is aware only that Wilson makes it to Gatsby's and then shoots him. But how does he alight upon Gatsby? It isn't until the closing chapter that Wilson's threatening confrontation with Tom Buchanan gets a hearing.

We cannot close out the discussion without drawing attention to some of the language. One of these noteworthy passages is the rather cryptic description of Gatsby in his very last moments of life. As has been my experience, many students will not know what to do with this relatively nebulous passage, especially since the sound of Wilson's gunshot is not the center of the death scene. Rather, it is Gatsby's own half-dreaming and despairing state of mind that claim the center. It is from Nick's own imaginings based upon what he, of all characters, knows to be true about Gatsby:

> I have an idea that Gatsby himself didn't believe it [Daisy's phone call] would not come, and perhaps he no longer cared. If that was true he must have felt that he had lost the old warm world, paid a high price for living too long with a single dream. He must have looked up at an unfamiliar sky through frightening leaves and shivered as he found what a grotesque thing a rose is and how raw the sunlight was upon the scarcely created grass. A new world, material without being real, where poor ghosts, breathing dreams like air, drifted fortuitously about . . . like that ashen, fantastic figure gliding toward him through the amorphous trees. (161)

The passage calls to mind at least more than one connection. Most directly, it is a scene in which nature is, again, infused with all the feelings of the brokenhearted or of the person for whom the world has lost its savor. The rose, a beautiful thing when you're in love, becomes "grotesque" in the eyes of the man who has lost everything, whether that be in the form of a lover or in the ability to find novelty in the world. Both are experiencing a kind of death. Gatsby's half-waking state of mind is then fused seamlessly with Wilson's. Wilson is a ghost of a man, just as Gatsby floats at the center of his pool with only the ghost of a once vital dream. In the abstract, the passage reflects the theme connected to Doctor T. J. Eckleburg, essentially a world in which God is not only relegated to a forgotten advertisement (or the refiguring of God as the man of big business), but is as ashen as the solemn dumping ground and that "fantastic figure gliding toward [Gatsby] through the amorphous trees."

With the deaths of Myrtle, Wilson, and Gatsby, the final words of the chapter read, "and the holocaust was complete" (162). Fitzgerald's **diction**, or choice of the word "**holocaust**," begs for interpretation. What is the **authorial intent**, if any? In leading students down this path, they will hopefully recognize that what we now associate with the word, holocaust, is still a ways into the future from where Nick now stands at the edge of Gatsby's pool. The origins of the word come from the Greek, meaning "whole" (holos) and "burning" (kaustos). It was associated with the burning of an individual's whole body, and often (but not always) alive. The victim could be a lamb, a piglet, a grown person or even a human child.

The question becomes: whose holocaust is it? Is it Gatsby's? If so, then what does he destroy? Himself? His own dreams? And why would he include George and Myrtle in the "sacrifice"? This is a slightly forced interpretation, which is one reason it makes more sense that it be Tom's holocaust. He reigns, while those who threatened to disrupt his comforts and security are now burned under the extreme heat on the last day of summer (Nor does this interpretation compete with the comparison to Icarus; in fact, it fulfills it.). As I and many others have said, Tom is **indirectly** responsible for all three deaths.

Tom's holocaust is not sacred at all, and it appeases nothing like a traditional, sovereign god. There is no show of piety or devotion to anything other than what Tom needs to sustain himself: his old money. Without it, he could never have married Daisy and wouldn't be able to save her from taking responsibility for Myrtle's accident. It is, thus, an anti-holocaust, a "hollow"caust, which makes Gatsby's sacrifice far more tragic than if he had just been a sacrificial lamb for the good of an ancient community. Instead, his exultant, striving spirit becomes a mere casualty of Tom's efforts to remain a "revolting" husband (chapter 7) and brutish playboy.

Character Foils: Gatsby is *not* unlike Myrtle Wilson (and her husband). Like Gatsby, for whom Dan Cody's yacht "represented all the beauty and glamour in the world" (100), Myrtle wants to be like those of Daisy's set or the fashionable movie stars featured in her favorite issues of "*Town Tattle* and a moving-picture magazine " (27). Gatsby, one might venture, is a more successful version of the Wilsons. While the youthful Gatsby uses his charm and charisma to figuratively hitch his sail to Dan Cody's yacht, Myrtle uses her sexuality to hitch an expensive ride with Tom Buchanan. But before some students superciliously judge Myrtle, as have mine, it is good to remind them of the typical post-suffrage woman, who still had little recourse if she wanted to move up in society, for while the 1920s was a sexual revolution of sorts, it was also an era in which strict conventions for women still loomed large under the tutelage of one's Victorian-era relatives, with whom these vital women of the "jazz age" could still have tea. Tom's bigoted commentary on both women and African Americans (12) upholds the resurgence of old influences.

Let's not forget, finally, that both Jay Gatsby and George Wilson lose each of their loves to the same man, Tom Buchanan. In this sense, both Wilson and Gatsby are ultimately failures; however, Gatsby, buoyed always by his great wealth and his visionary optimism, manages for a time to pose a threat to Tom. However, it would not be wrong to say that Gatsby inadvertently gives Tom nothing more than a chance to revitalize his feelings for Daisy through the thrill of a good old-fashioned duel. Tom wins the duel, both at the Plaza Hotel and in the end, for he will deliberately and successfully dodge the bullet meant for him, resulting in the mutual destruction of both of Tom's opponents. He effectively turns Daisy against Myrtle, as well, leaving only Daisy unscathed, but now completely dependent upon his money, power, and protection to escape responsibility for her hit-and-run accident.

It will be hard for *some* students to think of Tom as responsible for the death of Myrtle; Tom wasn't driving the yellow car, after all, and he was clearly upset by Myrtle's death. In a real-life courtroom, this accusation would never fly, but in literature it rings with the tones of poetic irony and satisfies the mind with flawless plot construction.

THE GREAT GATSBY

Character Foils: Whole and small-group activity

The term "character foil" comes from the practice of backing gems with foil in order to make them shine more brightly. The same can be done with two pieces of paper, one black, and one white. If you were to exchange the white for green, the black would not show up as well. If you were to exchange the black for brown, the white would not stand out as much.

For the most part, characters in a fictional story can be used in a similar way. The most obvious examples of character foiling come in the form of doubling, or doppelgangers, or two characters that are, in every way, completely opposite of one another. For example, in *The Strange Case of Dr. Jekyll and Mr. Hyde*, the former is gentlemanly, decorous and temperate. Mr. Hyde is the opposite; he is vulgar, debased and impulsive. When Mr. Hyde behaves impulsively, it makes Dr. Jekyll seem that much more temperate, and when Dr. Jekyll behaves with the care and refinement of a gentleman, he makes Hyde seem far more vulgar and debased. The two characters are, of course, the same person, but two sides of the same coin; the two identities become manifest as a split personality, and the perpetual juxtapositions of their respective activities continue to widen the gap between them.

But a character foil is not always so easily determined. It does not even have to consist of total opposites. Its chief function is to expose more clearly the traits and predicaments of each of the two characters. What are the character's similarities? What are their differences? Try this out with two characters from *The Great Gatsby*. Then see if you and a partner can identify two more characters whose experiences are parallel, but opposite. Let's begin, however, by comparing/contrasting Jay Gatsby and George Wilson as a class:

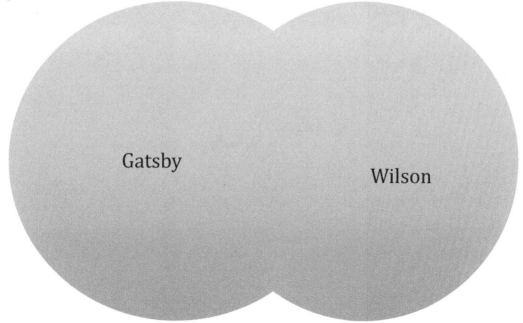

Character Foils

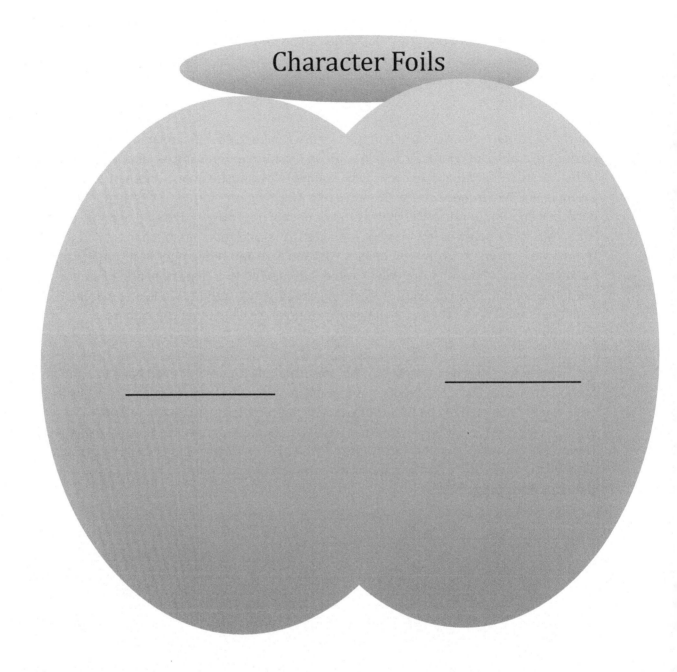

THE GREAT GATSBY

Scene from Chapter 8   **Wilson's Garage**

DIRECTIONS: As a whole class, or in a group of two or three, read the following adaptation from chapter eight. Then, discuss Wilson's reaction to Myrtle's death. How would you describe his state of mind?

Setting: It is long after midnight at George Wilson's garage. George Wilson is sitting inside rocking himself forward and back on the couch. His neighbor, Michaelis has stayed with him most of the night, along with various others. At about 3:00 a.m., it is now just Michaelis who is still with George. At this time, the quality of Wilson's incoherent muttering is changing, and he is growing quieter and beginning to talk.

George: I have a way of finding out who that yellow car belongs to. *(he pauses)* A couple of months ago she come from the city and her face was all bruised and her nose was swollen. *(hearing himself speak these words, he flinches and covers his face and cries out)* Oh, my God! . . . Oh, my God! *(George begins rocking back and forth again)*

Michaelis *(trying to distract George)*: How long have you been married, George? *(He walks over to George and lays a gentle hand on his shoulder)* Come on there, try and sit still and answer my question. How long have you been married?

George: Twelve years. *(George continues to rock and to look distraught and distracted)*

Michaelis: Ever had any children? Come on, George, sit still—I asked you a question. Did you ever have any children? *(He pauses, but George is not responding, and is still rocking)* Have you got a church you go to sometimes, George? Maybe even if you haven't been there for a long time? Maybe I could call up the church and get a priest to come over and he could talk to you, see?

George: *(staring straight ahead. He is still rocking.)* Don't belong to any.

Michaelis: *(he sits in a chair directly across from George, and attempts to make eye contact)* You ought to have a church, George, for times like this. You must have gone to church once. Didn't you get married in a church? Listen, George, listen to me. Didn't you get married in a church?

George: *(Sadly)* That was a long time ago. *(He stops rocking. Then the same half-knowing, half-bewildered look comes back into his faded eyes).* Look in the drawer there. *(George points at the desk in the room).*

Michaelis: Which drawer?

George: That drawer—that one. *(He points again)*

THE GREAT GATSBY

Michaelis opens the drawer nearest his hand. He pulls out a small, expensive dog-leash made of leather and braided silver. It is apparently new. Michaelis holds it up:

Michaelis: This?

George: *(He nods in the affirmative)* I found it yesterday afternoon. She tried to tell me about it, but I knew it was something funny.

Michaelis: You mean your wife bought it?

George: She had it wrapped in tissue paper on her bureau.

Michaelis: George. There could be many reasons she has the leash. Maybe she bought it for a friend? Maybe . . . I don't know . . . maybe it belongs to someone else, or

George: *(George interrupts Michaelis)* Oh, my God! . . . Oh, my God! . . . *(He begins rocking again, looking horrified)* Then he killed her. *(His mouth opens suddenly)*

Michaelis: Who did?

George: *(with chilling determination)* I have a way of finding out.

Michaelis: You're morbid, George. This has been a strain to you and you don't know what you're saying. You'd better try and sit quiet till morning.

George: *(quietly)* He murdered her.

Michaelis: *(looking at him incredulously)* It was an accident, George.

George: *(Wilson shakes his head from side to side, slowly. His eyes narrow and his mouth widens)* I know. . . . I'm one of these trusting fellas and I don't think any harm to NObody, but when I get to know a thing I know it. It was the man in that car. She ran out to speak to him and he wouldn't stop.

Michaelis: How could she of been like that?

George: She's a deep one. . . Ah-h-h----- *(He begins to rock again).*
Michaelis stands helplessly twisting the leash in his hand.

Michaelis: Maybe you got some friend that I could telephone for, George?
(George Wilson's glazed eyes turn toward the window as if looking toward the ash heaps. After a period of silence, George begins to speak slowly and deliberately.)

THE GREAT GATSBY

George: I spoke to her. I told her she might fool me but she couldn't fool God. I took her to the window. *(He stands up slowly and stares defiantly out the window. With an effort, he walks to the window and presses his face against it looking directly out at the billboard of Doctor T. J. Eckleburg.)*

George: *(Pause)* I took her to the window and I said 'God knows what you've been doing, everything you've been doing. You may fool me, but you can't fool God!'
(Standing behind him, Michaelis sees with shock that George is looking at the eyes of Doctor T. J. Eckleburg.)

George: God sees everything.

Michaelis: That's an advertisement.
(Michaelis turns away from the window, but George Wilson remains, his face close to the window pane, nodding into the twilight.)

End of Scene

THE GREAT GATSBY

Ch. 8: Post-Discussion QUEST Name_____

Part I: Vocabulary: Place each of the following vocabulary words in its correlating sentence. NOTE: *All* forms of the words will need to be changed (e.g. from adverb to adjective, etc.) in order to be used correctly in their sentences.

- A. Ravenously
- B. Unscrupulously
- C. Stratum
- D. Redolent
- E. Amorphous

1. The lighted candle burned _____ of clean linen.

2. The _____ politician took bribes.

3. The _____ dog inhaled its food.

4. The cloud floated by _____ as it was being chased by the wind.

5. The characters in *The Great Gatsby* are characterized partly by their _____ in society.

DIRECTIONS: Read the excerpt below and answer the following two questions:

"The track curved and now it was going away from the sun, which, as it sank lower, seemed to spread <u>itself</u> in benediction over the vanishing city where she had drawn her breath."

6. _____ What is the antecedent of "itself"?
    - A. The track
    - B. The sun
    - C. The city
    - D. benediction

7. _____ What literary device is being employed in the above passage?
    - A. Metaphor
    - B. Personification
    - C. Allegory: A device in which characters and events stand for abstract ideas, principles, or forces, so that the literal situation suggests a deeper symbolic meaning. A good example would be George Orwell's *Animal Farm*.
    - D. Apostrophe: A direct address to an inanimate object or an absent or deceased person: "Oh Moon, Why Art Thou Sad?"

THE GREAT GATSBY

DIRECTIONS: Answer the following questions on a separate sheet of paper:

8. Explain the **authorial intent** in the use of the word "holocaust" in the final sentence of chapter eight: "The holocaust was complete." What are the origins of the word "holocaust" and whose holocaust is it? Why?

9. Explain how two characters from *The Great Gatsby* could be considered **character foils**.

THE GREAT GATSBY

Chapter Nine: *The Great Gatsby*

Pre-Reading Journal Question:

- What should be a person's attitude toward the past, present, and future? Which should have the greatest focus: Past or present or future? Which should get the least focus? Explain or qualify your response.

Vocabulary Review: In chapter seven, you will encounter most of the following words. For each word, find its definition and write a sentence using the word correctly. Be sure there is enough information in your sentence so your teacher can tell that you understand *how* the word is used. **Do not simply repeat the meaning of your word in the sentence.** Identify its part of speech as written below (i.e., adjective, noun, verb, adverb). Also, be able to **decline or change each word's part of speech** as is required for the next QUEST. This pertains to the first seven words below:

- Surmise
- Superfluous
- Aesthetic
- Commensurate
- Obscurity
- Eluded
- Allusion (Literary Term)

Preview of Class Discussion:

1. Why does Nick take charge of Gatsby's funeral?

2. Who comes to Gatsby's funeral? Of those who did not come to the funeral, which ones did you fully expect to be there? Give reasons.

3. Do you agree with Wolfsheim when he says, "Let us learn to show our friendship for a man when he is alive and not after he is dead. . . . After that, my own rule is to let everything alone." Does this sentiment carry more or less value coming from Wolfsheim? Explain.

4. Why does Nick meet up again with Jordan? Why doesn't he get back together with her?

5. Why doesn't Nick tell Tom the truth, that Daisy was driving the "death car"? Find phrases that support your answer.

THE GREAT GATSBY

6. In the penultimate paragraphs of the novel, Nick meditates upon the Sound for one last time. The paragraph begins, "Most of the big shore places were closed now . . . ." What comparison is being made? What is the point of the comparison?

7. What does Nick mean when he says Gatsby's dream "was already behind him"? What does it mean to be "boats against the current"? Here are the famous final lines of the novel:

> He had come a long way to this blue lawn, and **his dream** must have seemed so close that he could hardly fail to grasp it. He did not know that **it was already behind him**, somewhere back in that vast obscurity beyond the city, where the dark fields of the republic rolled on under the night.
>
> Gatsby believed in the **green light**, the orgastic [*intensely pleasurable*] future that year by year recedes before us. It eluded us then, but that's no matter—to-morrow we will run faster, stretch out our arms farther. . . . And one fine morning—
>
> So we beat on, **boats against the current**, borne back ceaselessly into the past.

THE GREAT GATSBY

Ch. 9: Post-Reading, Pre-Discussion Quiz   Name_____

1. _____How does Mr. Gatz find out about Gatsby's murder?
   A. Nick calls to tell him about it.
   B. Wolfsheim calls him.
   C. He reads about it in the newspaper.
   D. The authorities contact him.

2. _____Where does Wilson get the idea to go to Gatsby to enact his revenge?
   A. He goes from garage to garage along his path to West Egg looking for the yellow car.
   B. He enters Tom's house in a threatening manner and Tom puts the blame on Gatsby, then tells Wilson where he can find Gatsby's house.
   C. He asks Gatsby's neighbors about who owns a yellow car, and they tell him and then point the way to Gatsby's house.
   D. He is led to Gatsby's house by some mysterious feeling, as if the hand of God had taken him there.

3. _____ Who attends Gatsby's funeral?
   A. Daisy
   B. Nick
   C. Wolfsheim
   D. Owl Eyes
   E. B and C
   F. B and D

4. _____ What seems to be of most concern to Klipspringer when he speaks to Nick on the phone?
   A. His record player.
   B. His tennis shoes
   C. The details surrounding Gatsby's murder.
   D. The day and time of the funeral.

5. _____ Why does Nick say that the story of the Great Gatsby is a story of the West?
   A. All of the main characters are Westerners (West of Ohio).
   B. Because America to the rest of the world is considered the West.
   C. Because Gatsby is from "West" Egg.
   D. Because the Eastern City of New York is beginning to reflect America's "Wild West" of gambling, saloons, and cheap women.

6. _____What does Nick realize primarily about Jordan and the Buchanans?
   A. That the rich get richer and the poor get children.
   B. That they are generally selfish, indulgent, and reckless.

C. That they are just ordinary people with dreams just like everyone else.
D. That they desperately need moral guidance, a system of beliefs akin to what religion offers.

THE GREAT GATSBY

CHAPTER NINE: Pre-Discussion Critical Summary for the Teacher

Literary Concept: Allusion

Chapter nine is deliberately anti-climactic, a precipitous downfall with no drama and no ceremony. Gatsby was, **in terms of the rarity of his spirit**, a god among mortals, but a god who will never be worshipped, revered, or even remembered. Only three people seem to recognize something of his value, and these are the same *disciples* (not including the employees) who attend his funeral: Nick, Mr. Gatz, and Owl Eyes. All the rest *betray* (biblical connotations intended) him by treating Gatsby's funeral as a major inconvenience. Wolfsheim, too, shirks his allegiance to Gatsby. In an impersonal note, he claims in one breath that the news of Gatsby has him completely "knocked down and out" but that he "cannot get mixed up in this thing now." He follows up with an afterthought about the funeral, but says he does not know the family, an indication that he won't be attending (166). If Wolfsheim says anything seemingly heartfelt and sincere, it is more likely that, in the words of Gatsby, "This is one of his sentimental days" (73). The sentimentalist cries more than he feels; and his tears dry up quickly.

The question of why no others show up for the funeral should sustain a lively classroom discussion. One answer might connect the no-shows to the weather, once again. During the fair-weather season of summer, when the champagne flows and musicians tap out their syncopated melodies, everyone flocks to Gatsby's like moths to a lantern and soak up his liquor. But when the host lays supine in a casket, he is a bore, a killjoy. Furthermore, coming out to a rainy funeral on a gray September day is depressing for those only interested in having a good time or in getting ahead. What might someone gain simply by paying tribute to a powerless corpse? The point is well taken, I hope: Gatsby is no longer in a position to do the commissioner or anyone else any more favors. Like Nick, the sound reader is likely to feel a kind of outraged sense of injustice for Gatsby; everyone deserves a memoriam, especially Gatsby, for he pursued the American dream heroically, even in light of his covert business operations; he had always loved a single woman and never cheated on her, even while she was married, a striking contrast to Tom; he was killed for a crime he did not commit; and his death was treated with no more regard than the crushing of an ant upon a sidewalk, which is to say life will go on as if he had never lived, unless Nick, himself, provides a fitting memoriam, or writes his book.

The most glaring absence is Daisy's. Of course, we discover from Nick's chance encounter with Tom that she perpetuated the notion that Gatsby was driving the "death car." Nor did she stop Tom from giving Wilson the necessary information that would lead him straight to Gatsby. She has much reason to be ashamed, for she now has plenty of blood on her hands. Going to Gatsby's funeral would have (or should have) evoked deep feelings of unbearable guilt. Nonetheless, Daisy is out of town and unreachable, safe from the consequences of her actions and able to behave as if her hit-and-run accident never occurred and Jay Gatsby never existed. And yet, she was

THE GREAT GATSBY

Gatsby's divine inspiration, and this is probably why her failure to pay tribute to him strikes one as worse than the combined betrayals of all others who wandered onto his lighted path.

Sadly, Mr. Gatz discovers his son's murder through an impersonal report in a Chicago newspaper and travels to West Egg for the funeral. He is solemn and helpless, with leaky eyes and of humble origins, truly an unlikely sire to a legend. He is, at once, grief stricken and proud of his son's accomplishments as he paces the halls of the Long Island castle, admiring tokens of "Jimmy's" material wealth (167-8). Mr. Gatz shows Nick one of Jimmy's old books (**Hopalong Cassidy**), a series about a fittingly romantic literary figure of the Old West. On one of the blank pages is scribbled a list of resolves very similar to something **Benjamin Franklin** wrote for himself (173). The **allusion** is deliberate. Franklin is considered America's first self-made man, the iconic figure who does not inherit his money and stance in the world but shapes them both out of the raw materials of his ingenuity, charm and talents. Indeed, by the age of forty, Franklin was as financially comfortable, educated, and as politically important as most of America's early aristocrats (e.g., Washington, Adams, Jefferson, Madison, Hamilton). Gatsby has striven to be more of a Franklin than a Buchanan.

As Nick's view of New York (and of the East) has been distorted, he begins to actively miss the small provincial towns of his youth. Nick realizes the drawbacks of these towns, with all of their righteous indignation and boring past times, for he once fled them for the excitement of the East. But the East is now more insidious to him than anything the "Middle West" might present. His illustration resembling the **religious paintings of El Greco** is a direct contrast to his Currier and Ives-style recollection of sleigh bells, street lanterns, and holly wreaths at Christmas (176). In essence, it is a visual representation of total indifference to human suffering, the opposite of the **Good Samaritan**. The woman on a stretcher might as well be a homeless man freezing to death at the feet of a bustling crowd, aimed everywhere and nowhere. Who is the man on the street? Who is the woman in the painting? It hardly matters. "No one knows . . . and no one cares" (176).

However, Nick is now determined in his own integrity. He will not leave town until he allows Jordan closure concerning their breakup. It is interesting that he has stopped grouping her with Tom and Daisy when he describes careless people. But Jordan will always be, by default, associated with the world Nick has come to see as morally distorted, and her final words do not make it any better: "It was careless of me to make such a wrong guess. I thought you were rather an honest, straightforward person. I thought it was your secret pride" (177).

Nick later encounters Tom on the street and refuses, at first, to shake hands with him. To appease Nick for giving Wilson Gatsby's home address, Tom insists that he had no choice but to tell "the truth" about Gatsby driving the car and that he too endured terrible suffering when he came across Myrtle's bag of dog biscuits: "I sat down and cried like a baby. By God it was awful—." Nick gives up trying to reason with Tom, for he'd have to tell him that Daisy was driving the car, and he is not confident that it would do any good. Nick realizes that Mr. Buchanan is an emotional infant who simply reacts on impulse, with little understanding of the consequences of his actions:

> I saw that what he had done was, to him, entirely justified. It was all very careless and confused. They were careless people, Tom and Daisy—they smashed up things and creatures and then retreated back into their money or their vast carelessness, or whatever it was that kept them together, and let other people clean up the mess they made. . . . I shook hands with him; it seemed silly not to, for I felt suddenly as though I were talking to a child. Then he went into the jewelry store to buy a pearl necklace—or perhaps only a pair of cuff buttons. (179)

The penultimate paragraphs on the final page of *The Great Gatsby* deserve intense analysis. Nick's trunk is packed and he is ready to leave the east. But before he does, he reclines once more upon Gatsby's beach to mediate upon the Long Island Sound. As the day darkens, only the outline of the trees across the waters is visible. Nick imagines what it must have been like for the Dutch explorers when they first beheld the island. Nick offers a telling description of a Dutch sailor standing "face to face for *the last time* in history with something *commensurate* to his capacity for wonder" [My Italics]. In sum, the arrival of the Dutch upon the shores of what would shortly become New Amsterdam was the last time the world was able to furnish the large-souled dreamer with anything equal to his sense of wonder. Centuries later, another dreamer would *come again*, but the world by this time would no longer reciprocate the breadth of his longings. Both the Dutch sailors and Gatsby reach toward the "green." For the sailors, that green moved them into an undiscovered country. But for Gatsby, there was nothing of substance left to grasp. Even as he stood there on the dock reaching out for Daisy's green light, the future had already receded into the past when great men endured (180).

> He did not know that it [his dream] was already behind him, somewhere back in that vast obscurity beyond the city, where the dark fields of the republic rolled on under the night. (180)

The Great Gatsby bears all of the traces of a modern novel, classed alongside the likes of Hemingway and Faulkner, where antagonists and protagonists are never neatly compartmentalized, but where God is effectively dead and nihilism pervades. However, Fitzgerald (or Nick) leaves us all with a bit of sobering hope, after all. Though the future moves constantly behind **us**, as do the waves against which **we** row, and though the modern world may not reflect the largeness of one's vision and hopes to discover something truly great (i.e. not the kind of "greatness" one would associate with 20th-century naked ambitions to gain wealth and prestige), we strive anyway, because the

THE GREAT GATSBY

search to be *truly* great is more important than actually fulfilling the dream, for at the height of its flowering, the dream begins to wilt:

> Gatsby believed in the green light, the orgastic future that year by year recedes before us, but that's no matter—to-morrow **we** will run faster, stretch out our arms farther. . . . And one fine morning—
> So we beat on, boats against the current, borne back ceaselessly into the past. [My Italics] (180)

THE GREAT GATSBY

Allusion

What is an **allusion**? It is a brief and non-specific or non-exact reference to a person, a place, or a thing of cultural or historical import. In an allusion, the reference is not explicit or named, and so the reader is expected to understand and apply the reference without any explanation.

Why an **allusion**? Just by associating a person, place, or thing with something of cultural or historical import, an author can create a desired, elevating (or demoting) association in the mind of the reader. For instance, watching an ant carry a large bee to its nest may not seem particularly revolutionary to most people. But if an author wanted the reader to see that this ant is actually doing something epically remarkable, the author might describe the ant's endeavors in Herculean terms or as Sisyphus. Most people know something about Greek legends, and this association, if done effectively, will place the anonymous ant in league with the likes of the Ancient Greek heroes and gods. The device in this case raises the impressiveness and value of the ant's pursuits significantly.

The young Jim Gatz's to-do list calls to mind chapter six of Benjamin Franklin's autobiography, in which Franklin attempts to become more virtuous. He makes several resolves that will help him to improve and not to let the days wear away in wasted talent. He includes both long-range and short-range goals. See the following website for a look at chapter six and Franklin's resolves:
http://www.usgennet.org/usa/topic/preservation/bios/franklin/chpt6.htm

1. In what ways are Franklin's resolves and Gatsby's resolves similar?
2. What is Franklin's claim to fame? What is his historical and cultural significance?
3. So, what is the possible, intended effect of the allusion to Franklin? How might this reflect upon Gatsby? Discuss this in a small group or as a class.
4. Find one other allusion in the chapter. Ferret out the purpose of its being there.

THE GREAT GATSBY

The Effect of a Comparison: The Paintings of El Greco (Domenicos Theotokopoulos)

Nick spends some time talking about his view of a distorted New York City. To create an illustration to help the reader understand what Nick has in mind, he describes a scene *in the style of a painting* by El Greco. Why El Greco? Go to the web address from the El Greco Foundation and learn a little bit about El Greco. Look through the paintings or scroll through the slideshow: http://www.el-greco-foundation.org/

Here are some questions to help you focus productively:

1. With what subject (e.g. nature, courtly life, romantic love, stories from the bible, etc.) is the artist mostly concerned?
2. How would you describe the figures in the paintings?
3. If you had to describe a tone or a mood in some of the paintings, what would it be?

Reread the passage where Nick describes his own version of an El Greco scene:

> In the foreground four solemn men in dress suits are walking along the sidewalk with a stretcher on which lies a drunken woman in a white evening dress. Her hand, which dangles over the side, sparkles cold with jewels. Gravely the men turn in at a house—the wrong house. But no one knows the woman's name, and no one cares. (176)

1. Can the scene as envisioned by Nick be at all compared to any of the scenes in El Greco's paintings?
2. Given what you have seen of El Greco's work, why would Nick choose him as the artist to paint the scene he has dreamed up in his mind?
3. Look at the online exhibition for The New York *Metropolitan Museum of Art* and find an artwork that you believe illustrates a major theme from *The Great Gatsby*. Write down the name of the artwork and the artist. Be ready to share the reasons for your choice. Here is the site address: http://www.metmuseum.org/collection/the-collection-online

THE GREAT GATSBY

Ch. 9: Post-Discussion QUEST   Name_____

Part I: Vocabulary: Place each of the following vocabulary words in its correlating sentence. NOTE: *Some* forms of the words <u>will need to be changed</u> (e.g. from adverb to adjective, etc.) in order to be used correctly in their sentences.

- Surmise
- Superfluous
- Aesthetic
- Commensurate
- Obscurity
- Eluded

1. Your salary will be _____ with your work experience and level of education.

2. An umbrella is _____ on a clear, sunny day.

3. John's remarks about the play were difficult to follow and _____.

4. The crafty criminal managed to _____ the police.

5. I can _____ from the appearance of your face that you must be very hot.

6. The arrangement of the furniture in this room is _____ pleasing to the eye.

7. _____What primary literary technique is Fitzgerald using when he sets the funeral on a gray, drizzly day?
   A. Foreshadowing: an indirect suggestion or clues that predict events yet to unfold in a story.
   B. Metaphor: a figure of speech that involves an implied or direct comparison between two relatively unlike things.
   C. Tone: The attitude or feeling that pervades a passage or given work, as determined by word choice, style imagery, connotation, sound, and rhythm.

8. <u>**Underline**</u> the *independent* clause in the sentence below (Even when . . .) from chapter 9.

9—11. Then, write each of the <u>subjects and verbs</u> of the *subordinate clauses* on the lines below. There are three:

THE GREAT GATSBY

(9). _____/_____ (10). _____/_____ (11). _____/_____

> Even when the East excited me most, even when I was most keenly aware of its superiority to the bored, sprawling, swollen towns beyond the Ohio, with their interminable inquisitions **which** spared only the children and the very old— even then it had always for me a quality of distortion.

12. In the sentence above, the word "which" is a relative pronoun relating back to a noun before it. What is the *antecedent* of the word "which"? Write your answer on the line below:

_____

In the same paragraph, there is a curious comparison between West Egg and an imagined night scene from a painting by El Greco. It reads,

> In the foreground four solemn men in dress suits are walking along the sidewalk with a stretcher on which lies a drunken woman in a white evening dress. Her hand, which dangles over the side, sparkles cold with jewels. Gravely the men turn in at a house—the wrong house. But no one knows the woman's name, and no one cares.

13. _____ What sort of comment is Nick making about West Egg when he uses this peculiar comparison? Choose the BEST answer.
   A. That West Egg is full of people who do not care about each other's welfare.
   B. That people in West Egg get drunk.
   C. That West Egg is a solemn and grave place.
   D. That the people of West Egg do not speak to each other.

Read the following passage from the final page of *The Great Gatsby* and answer the questions below:

> Most of the big shore places were closed now and there were hardly any lights except the shadowy, moving glow of a ferryboat across the Sound. And as the moon rose higher the inessential houses began to melt away until gradually I became aware of the old island here that flowered once for Dutch sailors' eyes— a fresh, green breast of the new world. Its vanished trees, the trees that had made way for Gatsby's house, had once pandered in whispers to the last and greatest of all human dreams; for a transitory enchanted moment man must have held his breath in the presences of this continent, compelled into an aesthetic contemplation he neither understood nor desired, face to face for the last time in history with something commensurate to his capacity for wonder.

THE GREAT GATSBY

    And as I sat there brooding on the old, unknown world, I thought of Gatsby's wonder when he first picked out the green light at the end of Daisy's dock. He had come a long way to this blue lawn, and his dream must have seemed so close that he could hardly fail to grasp it. He did not know that it was already behind him, somewhere back in that vast obscurity beyond the city, where the dark fields of the republic rolled on under the night.

14. _____ What OVER-ARCHING comparison is being made in the above passage?
    A. Gatsby's house AND human dreams
    B. The early Dutch sailors' contemplations and discoveries, AND Gatsby's wonder over the green light.
    C. Gatsby's house AND the dark fields of the republic that rolled on under the night.

15-17. What is the effect of the comparison above? How does it shape our interpretation of Gatsby?

18-25. Read the following excerpt from the final page of the novel. Then, respond to the questions below in a short essay. Use a separate sheet of paper.

    "Gatsby believed in the green light, the orgastic [intense and pleasurable] future that year by year recedes before us. It eluded us then, but that's no matter—tomorrow we will run faster, stretch out our arms farther. . . . and one fine morning—
    So we beat on, boats against the current, borne back ceaselessly into the past."

QUESTION: What does it mean for people in general to be "boats against the current borne back ceaselessly into the past"? What has this to do with Gatsby? Do the diction and tone of the final words of the novel lead us to the conclusion that Gatsby was a hero or that Gatsby was a failure? Defend your position. Organize your answers in a coherent response. Refer to specific word choices as you explain yourself.

THE GREAT GATSBY

Culminating Discussion Questions

1. Why is the novel called *The Great Gatsby*? Was Gatsby truly great? Explain.

2. How does the novel depict the American Dream in the 1920s? What does the novel seem to be suggesting about the values behind the American dream in this era? Where might they hold up? Where do they fail?

3. With which character do you most identify? Why?

4. Which character most deserves our empathy? Why?

5. Which theme, of all themes, does the novel develop the most? Show support for your response.

6. How is *The Great Gatsby* a modernist novel?

7. To what degree is the novel about Nick? To what degree is it about Gatsby? Explain.

THE GREAT GATSBY

The Great Gatsby can be seen in terms of the **five elements of plot construction**:

1. **The Exposition**: the introduction, in which the setting and main characters are established. Just as importantly, the reader is introduced to the conflict. *What is the conflict in The Great Gatsby? When is the reader aware of the conflict?*

2. **The Rising Action**: Once the reader has been introduced to the primary characters and the conflict has been introduced, things begin to get complicated. Tensions build as the conflict becomes more pronounced. The Rising Action culminates in the Climax. *When does the conflict in the novel start to get really complicated?*

3. **The Climax**: this element is similar to the detonation of an explosion. It might not always be this dramatic, but it occurs when the complications of the conflict build to its point of explosion. This is when the "truth" is revealed, and everything has been put "out on the table." One can also tell the climax by its aftermath or, to keep with the metaphor, by its fallout. Usually, the climax ushers on a dramatic turning point in the story. *What is the climax in novel?*

4. **The Falling Action**: After the point of climax, the story takes a new turn, because the truth is now out into the open and the character(s) must come to terms with what has been revealed. *What events would you count as being part of the falling action?*

5. **The Denouement**: This is where the story is concluded and all things are put into proper order or into proper perspective. It is often where the primary theme of the work comes back into focus, but with more clarity than before. *Where do you think the denouement in The Great Gatsby begins?*

THE GREAT GATSBY

Essay Topics

Choose <u>one</u> of the following essay topics and write a _____ paragraph essay with an introduction, thesis, and supporting paragraphs with topic sentences. End with a conclusion. Be sure to quote directly from the novel where appropriate; use only must-have quotes that help you support your thesis or topic sentences. Don't substitute quoting for writing, however; make sure your essay conveys a strong voice, <u>your</u> voice. Need help generating ideas for your essay?

1. Do some invention work. First, make a straight list of ideas, a list of supporting passages from the novel. Do some character mapping, diagramming, or use some other brainstorming approach;
2. Create a scratch outline with the thesis at the top;
3. Write your essay (criteria listed in the paragraph above).

Topics:

- Write an essay in which you examine the character of Jay Gatsby from the viewpoint of Nick Carroway. You should consider the novel's title: *The Great Gatsby*. Why do you think Fitzgerald chose this title for his novel?
- Write an essay in which you examine Nick Carroway as a trustworthy narrator of the story. Is he to be trusted to deliver a clear and fair account of the Buchanans and Gatsby during his Long Island summer? If so, then explain why we should trust his word. If not, then (obviously) why not?
- Write an essay in which you compare and contrast two characters that seem to be set up as doubles representing two parallel but differing worlds/visions, such as Gatsby and Tom, or Daisy and Myrtle.
- Write an essay in which you examine the importance of place in the novel and how it helps to reveal something important about the characters that inhabit these places, and/or an important theme. Talk specifically about West Egg, East Egg, the Valley of Ashes, and New York City.
- *The Great Gatsby* is full of symbols. Choose two or three significant symbols and write about how they animate our understanding of a character or an important theme. Symbols to consider would be the billboard advertisement, the weather, the seasons (summer and fall), the green light at the end of Daisy's dock. You might come up with others, such as the yellow car, the swimming pool, or even the dog collar. You should choose two or three symbols and not more. Combing the depths of a topic is always preferable to skimming the surface. Therefore, consider choosing only those two or three symbols that seem to be supporting a single theme, and work only with those.
- How does the novel depict the American Dream in the 1920s? What does the novel seem to be suggesting about the values behind the American dream in this era? Where might they hold up? Where do they fail? What is it that Gatsby fails to grasp? Is his vision tragic, or culpably flawed?

THE GREAT GATSBY

Twenty Post-Reading Creative Project Ideas

Standard (The project is meant to engage some higher order thinking skills)
Challenging (The project is meant to engage all higher order thinking skills):

Note: It is always possible to take a challenging project and make it predictable, clichéd and reflective of very little thought and effort. Conversely, a student can take a "standard" project and reinvent it or make it a masterpiece. These designations were made with the best of all possible scenarios in mind and with how well they, in their potential, are likely to stretch one's critical thinking. Some students may not yet have sufficiently developed capacities for abstractions, and so the standard projects should be a better fit. Nonetheless, one is always welcome to take a risk, if the motivation to do so is present. Moreover, all of the projects require imaginative thinking, hard work and the ability to keep a longer-term commitment.

1. Although some of the places in *The Great Gatsby* are/were real, others are fictional. However, real places, people, and events have direct correlations to fictional sites in the novel. For this project, you will create either a
   A. ***Gatsby* tour** for tourists visiting New York City in person. Or a
   B. ***Gatsby* virtual tour** using *Google Earth* and present it to the class.
   All of the places should have a clear connection to places in the novel. For some places, this will be easy. For others, you may need to do some research. For your tour, you'll need to create an attractive and inviting website approved by your teacher (the *Google Earth* component should be part of the page). One of the goals is to keep your website visitors clicking and discovering. For each stop on your tour, include an excerpt from the novel that mentions something about the place. If it connects to a fictional place mentioned in the novel, explain why you made your choice to put it on the tour. (*Standard*) This project may be done independently or with a single partner.

2. **Rewrite a passage** from the novel from the viewpoint of a character other than Nick Carroway. Show your reader that you really understand the character's interests and motivations, in harmony with the novel. Talk with your teacher about the length and other requirements of your piece. (*Standard*) This project should be done independently.

3. **Write a story** of your own invention, using original characters, and the time period and setting of your choice. However, do so using a <u>major</u> theme found in *The Great Gatsby*. Talk with your teacher about the length and plans for your piece. (*Standard*) This project should be done independently.

4. **Develop more fully one of the character's backstories**. The narration does some of this work, but not all. In some cases, Nick's retelling of Gatsby's backstory is little more than a gorgeously wrought plot description because he is retelling

THE GREAT GATSBY

what he heard and is not a witness to the event in the way he is in the rest of the novel where he is part of the action. So, what might you add? You may slow down the narration to add dialogue or develop a scene with your own descriptive storytelling. You might add some literary meat to the characters involved in Gatsby's past, such as Dan Cody; or you might create a backstory for Meyer Wolfsheim or Jordan Baker; you might develop the story of Tom and Daisy's honeymoon; or you might develop the backstory of how George and Myrtle got together or how Tom and Myrtle's relationship began. The possibilities are plentiful. Talk with your teacher about how you can take steps to accomplishing this project. (*Challenging*) This project should be done independently.

5. Write a **movie review** comparing and contrasting Francis Ford Coppola's 1974 film adaptation (Redford, Dern, Farrow, Waterston) of the novel with Baz Luhrmann's 2013 adaptation (DiCaprio, Mulligan, Maguire). Which film adaptation was truer to the novel? In which places did one or the other, or both, depart from Fitzgerald's story? Which one took more artistic liberties? Were these liberties fitting and effective? Did they enhance the story? For whom? Or did they, at any point, compromise something that is essential to understanding Gatsby's story? What are the positives, and what are the negatives of both films? What did you think of the casting? Were the actors' performances fitting for their respective characters? (e.g., Redford versus DiCaprio, or Farrow versus Mulligan) Defend your assertions with good reasoning and quotes from the novel and film(s). (*Challenging*) This project should be done independently.

6. **Research book reviews of *The Great Gatsby*,** from the date when it was first published until about thirty or forty years later. **Write an essay** summarizing (A) its review history, detailing how well or poorly it was received at first to (B) reasons why it went out of circulation and, finally, (C) the reasons for why it was reissued and the public's response during all of these phases. Include a works cited with your essay, which means you'll need to quote the words of various reviews. There is an excellent collection of historical reviews of the novel throughout the decades called *F. Scott Fitzgerald: The Great Gatsby,* edited by Nicolas Tredell from Columbia University Press. See your instructor for specific requirements. (*Standard*) This is an independent project.

7. **Create a *Fakebook* page** of either one of the characters from the novel or a real person upon which one of the novel's characters might have been based. Make it as biographically complete as possible and edit thoroughly. Exchange posts and comments with the other characters with *Fakebook* pages. Stay true to the time period as much as possible, even though the electronic approach is, admittedly, highly anachronistic. (*Standard*) This project should be done independently.

8. Create a **photo album/scrapbook** for one of the characters from the novel or for F. Scott Fitzgerald, himself. For the characters, read the descriptions in the novel very carefully to get a sense of their interests and experiences, both 'present' and past. For Fitzgerald, read biographical information from reputable sources. Include such items as symbolic trinkets, memorabilia, letters, newspaper clippings, and pictures. Try to use at least three primary sources along with your collection. For Fitzgerald, you should increase your number of primary sources to seven, as there are plenty of sources out there on him. Your album/scrapbook should be chronological, should include a bibliography or works cited, and a process paper. Talk to your instructor about specific length and total source requirements. (*Standard*) This project should be done independently.

9. Create an attractive and informative **bulletin board or multi-dimensional museum exhibit** on the novel's historical context. Your exhibit should include a thesis statement, pictures, short excerpts from the novel and a few primary sources, as well, including old newspaper articles. Here's a link to United States newspaper archives get you started: http://chroniclingamerica.loc.gov/ .

    This project is meant to be highly visual, so do not overwhelm the viewer by displaying too much writing or with writing that is hard to read. Any writing you include needs to be absolutely essential to supporting your thesis statement. You can make this display as striking as you desire. Use your creative imagination to make visitors and classmates want to study and admire it. Include a works cited or bibliography and display it. See your instructor for guidance and other specific requirements. (*Standard*) This project should be done independently or with a single partner.

10. Write an **"exclusive" interview** with one or more of the characters from the novel. You could do this as a sort of Oprah Winfrey interview or as a therapist behind "closed doors." Perform it in front of the class or record it as a podcast or on video. Make your questions deep and probing, while remaining true to the character(s); this way, you help to illuminate his or her side of the story. See your instructor for specific requirements. (*Standard*) This project should be done with a partner.

11. Create a 7-to-10 minute **original stage performance**

    (A) highlighting a theme or
    (B) a character or
    (C) a relationship between two characters from the novel, or
    (D) the story of Fitzgerald's writing life.

THE GREAT GATSBY

Whatever you choose, you must use a variety of sources and media. For instance, you would likely perform several roles, with a mere change of hats, as the narrator who delivers the introduction and thesis statement, and as one or more (rotating) characters from the novel. In your performance, you should quote or read excerpts from primary sources, such as letters, the novel, and/or relevant newspaper articles. For media, you might consider playing, singing, or simply using music from the time period, or even video footage from the era. There is plenty of footage on the Internet showing both Scott and Zelda, together, as well as of people out and about in New York City in the 1920s.

To see fully actualized performances of this type, go to http://www.nhd.org/StudentProjectExamples.htm and scroll down until you see the "performance" category. Keep in mind that these are nationally winning performances and are unusually ambitious. Use them, therefore, as a paradigm and for inspiration. Talk to your teacher about the requirements for your performance. Just cutting the length to 7 minutes can help to make such a project much less intimidating. (*Challenging*) This project can be done independently, with a partner or in a group of no more than three people.

12. Create a **1920s-style silent film** about one of the characters in the novel. Choose for your story a few moments from the character's past, as described in the novel. You may embellish the scene to make it fuller than it was described in the novel. However, make sure you help the viewer to understand better your character's 'present' motivations by revealing the past. Try to choose a character that is not very sympathetic, and get your audience to see him or her much more complexly than before. Interesting choices with plenty of potential would be the backstories of Tom Buchanan, Meyer Wolfsheim, George Wilson and, *especially*, Myrtle Wilson. (*Standard*) This project should be done in a group of no more than four people.

13. Create a **podcast interview** with F. Scott Fitzgerald very much like *The Thomas Jefferson Hour* with Clay Jenkinson. First, one would interview Fitzgerald, himself, as played by the expert, as played by you or your partner. Then, one would interview the expert as him/herself (not as Fitzgerald), who knows all about Fitzgerald's life, writing habits, and interests. If this seems confusing, listen to one of the episodes of *The Thomas Jefferson Hour* to understand the idea: http://www.jeffersonhour.com/listen.html . Your podcast does not need to be as long, however, as Jenkinson's. Be sure to ask questions that are somewhat deep and probing. See your teacher for further instructions and guidance. (*Challenging*) This project should be done in a group of two.

14. **Courtroom Trial** or **Traditional Lincoln-Douglas Style Debate**: Who is responsible for the downfalls of Gatsby and the Wilsons? Is it: Gatsby? Daisy? Tom? In two groups of two, choose a character to defend or prosecute. One might try to

show that Tom is fully at fault. But the other team may argue only that blame cannot be placed upon Tom. Both groups will act as teams of **literary lawyers**. As two teams of lawyers, you will work separately to shore up the strongest possible case to defend your position.

The showdown will occur in a **courtroom trial** or a **formal debate** in front of the class. You will need two or more volunteers to play the Judge, Tom, Daisy, Gatsby, or any other characters you intend to put on the stand (you'll need to prep them or provide them with a script of what you want them to say). Evidence and witness responses must be rooted in the novel and not invented. Take into account, also, the expectations for married women during the 1920s. Quote liberally from the novel. The students not involved will be your jury and must consider (in their rendering of the case's outcome) whether or not you stayed true to the novel's depictions or suggestions concerning the motivations, interactions and experiences (past and present) of these characters. (*Challenging*) This project requires four people. Witnesses and the judge are created out of volunteers from the classroom.

15. Nick talks about the "foul dust" that preyed upon Gatsby. The dust might be said to symbolize the press, which constantly pursues Gatsby. For example, in the opening of chapter six, a reporter knocks on Gatsby's door as part of a private investigation into "contemporary legends such as the 'underground pipe-line to Canada.'" Write up a **collection of original, fictional newspaper articles** reporting on Gatsby's involvements with his alleged secret operations, socialites who frequent his parties, and the tragic demises of George and Myrtle Wilson, as well as Gatsby, himself. Look at old newspaper articles from the 1920s to get an idea of a report of this kind would read. Choose and print a few *real* articles from the same time period to juxtapose with your original, *fictional* reports; you can arrange the entire collection chronologically. This project can be done by one or two people (at most).

    A few real persons and real events you might investigate include:
    - *Black Sox Scandal* (This refers to the fixing of the 1919 World Series)
    - *George Remus* (an inspiration for Gatsby; he was a renowned bootlegger who threw large parties at his mansion in Cincinnati; he also murdered his opportunistic wife and went to prison for it.)
    - *Arnold Rothstein* (the alleged inspiration for Meyer Wolfsheim)
    - *Teapot Dome Scandal* (Warren G. Harding administration, signifying the corruption rampant in the 1920s)
    - *Yankee Stadium* (It was constructed in 1922)
    - *William Desmond Taylor* (Movie director whose 1922 murder was sensationalized in newspapers; it is still a cold case.)
    - *Prohibition* (or the passing of the 18th Amendment)

THE GREAT GATSBY

- ***Women's Suffrage*** (or the passing of the 19th Amendment)
- ***World War I***

Here's a link to United States newspaper archives get you started: http://chroniclingamerica.loc.gov/ .

Although you'll need to embellish your reports in order to give them substance, be sure to report on events or material mentioned in the novel. See your instructor for length requirements and required number of entries. (*Challenging*)

16. Have you ever seen one of those birthday present nostalgia books, DVDs or CDs reviewing all of the major events and past times during the year of a person's birth? Here's a link to a publishing company that produces them: http://www.nostalgiapublishing.com/birthday-gifts.html

    Your job will be to pretend you are Daisy Buchanan creating a **nostalgia project** for her daughter, Pammy. In chapter one of the latest Scribner edition, Daisy's daughter is three-years-old, but in other places there is the suggestion that she is younger than that: two-years-old. Whichever age you choose is fine. The date of novel's setting is the summer of 1922, which places Daisy's daughter's birth at 1919 or 1920. OR: You may simply choose the year of the novel's setting and offer it as a birthday commemoration for the novel. Include in your nostalgia items a description of major political events, famous movies, clothing styles, sporting events, Nobel prize, powerful people, etc. Include a works cited of primary sources. This is a standard project and should be accomplished by one or two persons at most.

17. Create a ***Gatsby*** **game** that is unique, fun and challenging. Include categories and at least two levels of difficulty for each category. Categories might include: characters, words between characters, literary devices, vocabulary, the author, themes, setting, and historical context. (*Standard*) This project can be accomplished with one, two, or three people (at most).

18. **Create a cartoon of one of the passages in the novel**. You could do this as an old-fashioned cartoon strip or in a Powtoon (or something like it). A great scene for this might be from chapter seven where Myrtle is hit by Gatsby's car. As this project needs to involve an academic component, be sure to focus intensely upon the reactions of the characters to the accident. Each reaction says something very important about the characters. It says much about Tom, Daisy, Gatsby, Nick, Jordan, Wilson, and even Myrtle (whose death in metaphorical terms says something about why she can no longer thrive in the world). Creating the "correct" emotion on each of the character's faces will look a bit like a caricature in a freeze frame, but it will help your classmates pay attention to

those details they may have missed beyond the gruesome death scene. (*Standard*) This project could be accomplished with one or two people.

19. **Multi-Sensory Imagery Project: Close Textual Analysis of a Passage from the Novel** (*Challenging*): With a partner, you will select a passage of *about* <u>one page</u> from the novel and prepare a thorough analysis. The passage should be packed with enough literary devices and meaning to make the objective attainable. You will be responsible for ____ minutes of the class period during which time you will present your work. To ensure that you will remain as close to the presentation time frame as possible, practice repeatedly, time your presentation, and maximize your use of time to include as much intellectual substance as possible. Again, this project should be accomplished with no more than two people.

Requirements:

A. For use in oral presentation: One double-spaced copy of your _____-page analysis copied for your teacher. Your analysis should include thematic or philosophic overtones and undertones, literary devices, interesting choice and usage of diction, syntax (word arrangement), alliteration, hyperbole, imagery, irony, and everything that might contribute to the passage's tone and meaning. <u>Don't simply point out devices</u>; <u>explain how they work together to contribute to the passage's meaning.</u>

B. Physical Representations of imagery (Use three or more of the following to contribute to the class's understanding of your analysis).
   1. Sight -- visual aide: poster, sculpture, painting, diorama...
   2. Sound -- musical representation, memorized dramatic recitation, sound interpretation, sound effects...
   3. Taste -- food, drink...
   4. Smell -- scents...
   5. Touch -- cloth, wood, sand, etc...

Here are some tips for writing a great **Analysis**:
   1. Consider the passage's placement in the chapter and placement in the novel. Why is it there? What is the likely purpose for this?
   2. Describe how all of the following affect meaning. All passages of Fitzgerald's writing employ purposeful uses of diction and syntax, but does yours employ plentiful instances of figurative language? If your passage is extremely lean on imagery, consult with your teacher; you may be overlooking something, or it *may* be time to choose another passage:

THE GREAT GATSBY

- figurative language (imagery connected to as many of the five senses as possible: sight, sound, smell, touch or feeling, taste)
- diction (word choice)
- syntax (word arrangement)
- other literary devices? (hyperbole, irony, comparisons, juxtappositions, etc.)

20. (Group Project of no more than three) Throw a **Gatsby Theme Party**. (*Standard*) Use your creativity and a love of the culinary arts to achieve this; you can make this project seem like a boring afterthought or really make it fun, memorable and informative for all. It's not a particularly intellectual assignment, but will take commitment, abundant imaginative creativity, an interest in showing people a good time, and hours spent creating a few little multi-sensory masterpieces (Keep in mind the cost potential for this kind of project!). If that description sounds like it was written with you in mind, this is one to try! And . . . *now* . . .

    Here's **your** "to do" list:
    A. Create an invitation to your party at least two weeks ahead of your event. Include the usual "Where, When, and How" information. Make your invitation reflective of the Gatsby theme. Include what it is you need each attendee to do;
    B. Make available the necessary connections students need in order to perform their roles (e.g. ideas for to get or make *inexpensive* costumes and how to attain them, etc. This could mean picking up the phone and inquiring.);
    C. Bring food and drink associated with *The Great Gatsby* and its themes;
    D. Create a menu with an explanation of how the food connects to the novel (including direct quotes from the novel).
    E. Plan to play music that has direct connection to the novel and to the time period. Be ready to explain this in a creative way (e.g., During the party, you could play a *Name That Tune!* game with the class; but consider whether you might provide a selection of possible answers/song titles, since the music is not contemporary to your generation.);
    F. Decorate the room in ways that are reflective of the novel, of its themes, its symbols, recurring motifs, characters, etc. Again, you could make the students/attendees guess the relevance of each decoration and offer prizes (just a thought). Consider whether you want to hold the party in the classroom or if you'd rather use another, more fitting, space on campus. If the latter, be sure you set this up with your teacher about two weeks ahead of time.
    G. Other possibilities:

THE GREAT GATSBY

1) Include a photographer (There is a photographer someone could play from chapter two of the novel); consider, also, a journalist ferreting out the truths behind Gatsby legends and gossip.
2) Film Footage (to take footage of the party and to produce the film in vintage 1920s style, sped up, black & white, with dubbed 1920s music, etc.).
3) Show a movie that was popular anywhere from 1920-to-1922.

Instruct each attendee to:

- Choose a famous person from the 1920s or a character from the novel, *The Great Gatsby* (no one else may have your role). Each classmate will take on this person's persona by imitating him/her, arriving at the party in character (including a fitting costume) and staying in character for the duration. If anyone asks you your name, give them your character's name, not your own. If you are Charlie Chaplin, however, you may answer in pantomime."
- Bring a description of the person or character with the name underneath and a two-or-three sentence biography. Pin or tape the description to a display featuring all of the roles.
- Bring a few business cards to offer people during conversation. Include a tagline.
- Do something characteristic of your character or person. For instance, if you are Billy Holiday, you should consider singing. If you are a gangster, a gambler or bootlegger, you should perform some caper typical of your character.

Here are possible roles:

Men:

- Jay Gatsby
- Tom Buchanan
- Nick Carroway
- Meyer Wolfsheim
- George Wilson
- The photographer from chapter two of the novel (see below)
- F. Scott Fitzgerald
- Charles Chaplin
- Buster Keaton
- Benny Goodman
- Douglas Fairbanks
- Ernest Hemmingway
- Al Capone

THE GREAT GATSBY

- Arnold Rothstein
- George Remus

Women:
- Zelda Sayre Fitzgerald
- Genevra King
- Mary Pickford
- Clara Bow
- Gertrude Ederle
- Billie Holiday
- Greta Garbo
- Bessie Smith
- Daisy Buchanan
- Jordan Baker
- Myrtle Wilson

A Classroom Guide to *The Great Gatsby* Answer keys

Page 6, Socio-political and historical context:
1. A
2. C
3. B
4. C
5. D
6. C
7. D
8. C
9. D
10. F
11. E
12. Women granted right to vote. Ratified on Aug. 18, 1920. Possible answers include giving women a voice in U.S. democracy; decrease in child mortality rates; uptick in education enrollment; led eventually to women running for political office.
13. Outlawed manufacture, sale, & transportation of alcohol. Ratified on Jan. 16, 1919. Possible answers include organized crime; deaths from bathtub gin; loss of sources of income; aggressive resurgence of the KKK, which blamed immigrants for criminal activity.

Page 9, About the Author Quiz:
1. C
2. C
3. A
4. C
5. A
6. B
7. C
8. C
9. D
10. B
11. C
12. B
13. B
14. C
15. C

Page 14, Ch. 1 Post-Reading, Pre-Discussion Quiz:
1. B
2. D
3. E
4. A
5. B
6. D
7. C
8. D

Page 24, Ch. 1, Post-Discussion Quest
1. C
2. D
3. E
4. B
5. A
6. Responses will vary. For possibilities, read the teacher's commentary for chapter 1.

Page 26, Ch. 2, Post-Reading, Pre-Discussion Quiz:
1. C
2. A
3. C
4. B
5. B
6. D
7. B

Page 30, Ch. 2, Post-Discussion Quest
1. D
2. C
3. E
4. A
5. B
6. Responses will vary. For possibilities, read the teacher's commentary for chapter 2.

Page 33, Ch. 3, Post-Reading, Pre-Discussion Quiz
1. D
2. C
3. D
4. C
5. B
6. A
7. D
8. B
9. A
10. A

Page 39, Ch. 3, Post-Discussion Quest
1. I
2. H
3. M
4. K
5. L
6. N
7. A
8. D
9. J
10. E
11. B
12. C
13. B

A Classroom Guide to *The Great Gatsby* Answer keys

14. A
15. Responses will vary. For possibilities, read the teacher's commentary for chapter 3.

Page 44, Ch. 4, Post-Reading, Pre-Discussion Quiz
1. False
2. True
3. True
4. False
5. False
6. C
7. C
8. C
9. D
10. A

Page 51, Ch. 4, Post-Discussion Quest
1. A
2. E
3. B
4. D
5. C
6. Responses will vary. For possibilities, read the teacher's commentary for chapter 4.

Page 54, Ch. 5, Post-Reading, Pre-Discussion Quiz
1. Gatsby is distracted and nervous, almost ready to abort the entire plan to connect with Daisy.
2. Gatsby is elated, almost lightheaded. He can hardly believe Daisy is in his house. "He was consumed with wonder" and "running down like an overwound clock."
3. Daisy "cries stormily" into the shirts. She says she has never seen "such beautiful shirts before."
4. Now, after having made the connection with Daisy in person, the green light has been reduced to its more mundane proportions. Nick wonders if Gatsby's feelings will quickly die out after such a big build-up to his reunion with Daisy. Will the dream, symbolized by the green light, still have as much meaning for him?
5. It is raining.

Page 58, Ch. 5, Post-Discussion Quest
1. B
2. A
3. D
4. C
5. A
6. D

7. A
8. B
9. A
10. C
11. Tactlessly
12. Rendered
13. Vitality
14. Confounding
15. Gravely
16. Responses will vary. For direction, see teacher commentary for chapter 5.

Page 61, Ch. 6, Post-Reading, Pre-Discussion Quiz
1. Gatsby's real story is that he was born as James Gatz to shiftless farmers in North Dakota, dropped out of college and made his fortune after meeting multi-millionaire, Dan Cody. In the false story, Gatsby is born wealthy and attends Oxford. Says he is from San Francisco but erroneously calls it the "Middle West."
2. Dan Cody was a self-made multi-millionaire with a yacht. He inspired Gatsby's desire to become rich and to live opulently. His alcoholism also inspired Gatsby to avoid alcohol.
3. Daisy was unimpressed with the West Eggers at Gatsby's party. She thought they were tactless and overstated in all ways.
4. Gatsby's criterion was pinned entirely upon Daisy's approval.
5. Gatsby responds, "Why of course you can!"

Page 65, Ch. 6, Post-Discussion Quest
1. E
2. F
3. C
4. H
5. G
6. B
7. D
8. A
9. D
10. B

Page 69, Ch. 7, Post-Reading, Pre-Discussion Quiz
1. B
2. D
3. C
4. A
5. C
6. A

117

A Classroom Guide to *The Great Gatsby* Answer keys

Page 74, Ch. 7, Post-discussion Quest
1. C
2. G
3. A
4. F
5. D
6. E
7. B
8. C
9. A
10. C

Page 77, Ch. 8, Post-Reading, Pre-Discussion Quiz
1. True
2. True
3. False
4. False
5. True
6. B
7. D
8. C
9. G
10. F

Page 88, Ch. 8, Post-Discussion Quest
1. Redolently
2. Unscrupulous
3. Ravenous
4. Amorphously
5. Strata
6. B
7. B

8 & 9. Responses will vary. For possibilities, read the teacher commentary for chapter 8.

Page 92, Ch. 9, Post-Reading, Pre-Discussion Quiz
1. C
2. B
3. F
4. B
5. A
6. B

Page 100, Ch. 9, Post-Discussion Quest
1. Commensurate
2. Superfluous
3. Obscure
4. Elude
5. Surmise
6. Aesthetically
7. C
8. . . . . even then it had always for me a quality of distortion.

9. East / excited
10. I / was aware
11. Inquisitions / spared
12. Inquisitions
13. A
14. B

15—17. Responses vary. See the teacher's commentary for chapter 9.

18—25. Responses vary. See the teacher's commentary for chapter 9.

Made in the USA
Coppell, TX
03 March 2022

74384814R00066